CONFIDENTLY CARING FOR AGING PARENTS

NINE STRATEGIES TO MINIMIZE THE OVERWHELM
OF YOUR PARENTS' NEEDS, SAFEGUARD YOUR
FINANCES, AND IMPROVE FAMILY QUALITY OF LIFE

KIM LIVINGSTON

TABLE OF CONTENTS

INTRODUCTION

At the heart of each family lies a story woven with love, resilience, and the bond between generations. Meet Sam's parents, Mike and Kay—a couple whose remarkable journey of adventure, wisdom, and devotion captured the essence of what it means to live fully and love deeply.

Their story begins with the sound of tires on the road as Mike and Kay embark on cross-country adventures that span from the sun-kissed shores of Florida to the majestic vistas of California. Each mile was not just a journey but an opportunity to create cherished memories filled with laughter, discovery, and the heartwarming embrace of family bonds. Their journey was about the physical distance and the emotional depth they shared, making their story relatable and touching.

Yet, amidst the backdrop of their travels, quiet strength and wisdom defined their every step. Mike and Kay's commitment to financial prudence mirrored their approach to life— thoughtful, deliberate, and grounded in values that transcended mere possessions. Theirs was a journey guided not by fleeting desires but by the enduring principles of responsibility and stewardship, a unique path that resonates with many caregivers.

Their story took an unexpected turn as retirement beckoned, and the years unfurled like pages in a well-worn book. Kay's diagnosis of type 1 diabetes cast a shadow of uncertainty, presenting challenges that tested their resolve and bound them even closer together.

In the face of adversity, Mike became her unwavering guardian, a beacon of strength and support, inspiring hope in moments of vulnerability. Their journey was not without its trials, but their resilience and determination shone through, inspiring others to face their challenges with courage.

As the sands of time continued to shift, new challenges emerged, casting shadows on the horizon. Kay's health battles intensified, and Mike, too, faced his struggles with grace and dignity. It was a journey marked by highs and lows, triumphs and setbacks, but one thing remained constant: their unwavering love and the unbreakable family bonds.

Join us as we journey through the tapestry of their lives, exploring the depths of resilience, the power of love, and the enduring legacy of two souls intertwined in a dance of life, loss, and the beauty of what it means to care for one another.

Your Road Map to Caregiving: Navigating Transitions with Compassion and Self-Care

Embarking on a new caregiving journey can feel overwhelming, but you're not alone. Kim provides practical strategies and heartfelt advice to help you confidently and compassionately navigate this transition. Here's a glimpse of what Kim offers:

- **Assess your situation:** Understand needs, evaluate aspects, and be well-prepared for the road ahead.
- **Create a care plan:** Customize caregiving to meet loved ones' needs; Kim creates a plan.
- **Seek support:** Contact family, friends, and caregivers for crucial support.
- **Practice self-care:** Don't lose yourself along the way. Kim offers tips for prioritizing well-being through relaxation and rejuvenation.
- **Set boundaries:** Understand why establishing boundaries is crucial for maintaining balance and avoiding burnout.
- **Stay organized:** Find order in eldercare. Kim offers tools for managing caregiving responsibilities and organizing information.
- **Seek professional help:** Know who and what you can turn to. Kim assists in accessing healthcare, legal resources, and support systems.

Kim's book, *Confidently Caring for Aging Parents*, offers practical advice and personal anecdotes to empower caregivers. It guides readers through assessing their situation, creating care plans, seeking support, practicing self-care, setting boundaries, and staying organized. By following the guidance, caregivers can confidently navigate their journey with compassion and resilience, ensuring the well-being of their aging parents while prioritizing self-care and fulfillment.

Transitioning to Your New Caregiving Role

- **Accept and self-reflect:** Acknowledge your new role and reflect on your strengths and limitations.
- **Seek support and resources:** Contact family, friends, or support groups and research local resources.
- **Establish boundaries and prioritize self-care:** Set boundaries, prioritize well-being, and incorporate self-care.
- **Educate yourself and plan:** Learn about your parent's condition and create a care plan.
- **Communicate openly and compassionately:** Maintain open communication with aging parents.
- **Practice flexibility and adaptability:** Embrace flexibility and be kind to yourself.
- **Celebrate small victories and practice gratitude:** Cultivate gratitude for caring for aging parents and the lessons learned.

It is important to remember that caregiving is a long-term commitment, not a short-term task. You can navigate this journey with grace and strength by prioritizing self-care, seeking support, and approaching the role with compassion and resilience. You are capable, you are valued, and you are not alone. Take each step with courage and compassion, knowing that you are making a difference in the lives of your aging parents and your own.

The Power of the C-C-C Care Approach

Here's something that could make a difference in your care-giving journey: the C-C-C Care Approach. It is about boosting communication, coordination, and collaboration among caregivers, leading to better care quality, less stress, and improved well-being for you and your aging loved ones. By reading this book and using these strategies, you can:

- attain a harmonious lifestyle while effectively aiding aging parents.
- navigate the emotional and practical facets of caregiving without succumbing to overwhelm.
- elevate personal well-being by managing stress and establishing healthy boundaries.
- enhance communication abilities to better engage with parents and healthcare professionals.
- develop financial plans that safeguard your and your parents' financial futures.
- elevate the overall quality of life for yourselves and your aging parents through compassionate care.
- cultivate a network of supportive resources and relationships to alleviate the weight of caregiving.
- strategically plan for the future, ensuring parents' needs are met without compromising personal aspirations.
- foster a positive and nurturing atmosphere for the entire family despite the challenges of aging.

Navigating the C-C-C Approach to Confidently Care for Aging Parents

Embarking on caring for aging parents can feel overwhelming. Still, with the C-C-C Care Approach, you'll gain the confidence and tools to navigate this path gracefully and resiliently. Here's how it works:

- **Embrace your new role:** Step into your caregiving role clearly and purposefully.
- **Prioritize your parents' health:** Dive into practical ways to support your parents' health needs.
- **Nurture your well-being:** Understand that caring for yourself is as important as caring for your parents.

Navigating the caregiving journey can be daunting, but with the proper support and strategies, you can navigate it gracefully and resiliently. Embrace the guidance this book offers, and know you're not alone. Together, we can confidently care for our aging parents while prioritizing our well-being and finding fulfillment in the journey.

1

PREPARING FOR YOUR NEW CAREGIVING ROLE

From a young age, Sam was determined never to place his parents in a nursing home, and he was unwavering in his decision. During a family meeting, we devised plans to assist Mike and Kay, and the discussion unfolded smoothly.

Although they initially declined our offer, they eventually recognized our readiness to pause our lives to support them, leading to their acceptance. They then guided us through their important documents, like insurance policies, financial records, investments, and emergency funds, demonstrating their meticulous preparation.

However, the emotional weight of the situation hit us after we concluded the practical aspects of the meeting. Acknowledging the shift in dynamics, where we would need to oversee and care for Sam's parents, was particularly challenging for Sam and me, even more so than for Mike and Kay. It is tough to grapple with the impending role reversal, but it is the path we have committed to navigate together.

IT'S YOUR TURN

Caring for aging parents is a profound, rewarding, and daunting experience. It is a journey that is fueled by love and dedication. It's also a leap into the unknown, accompanied by waves of emotions.

Caregiving isn't only about practical tasks and navigating the emotional roller coaster ahead. There will be moments of joy, frustration, laughter, and tears. However, you'll make a meaningful difference in your parents' lives through it. Take a breath, knowing you're not alone on this journey.

THINGS TO CONSIDER BEFORE BECOMING YOUR PARENTS' CAREGIVER

Choosing to become your parents' caregiver is a deep and often complex decision. It requires careful consideration and preparation as you navigate the challenges and responsibilities of supporting your parents as they age. Before taking on this role, there are several important factors to consider, for example:

- **Know your capabilities:** Take a moment to assess your abilities and limitations. Be realistic about your emotional and physical preparedness for caregiving.
- **Understand your parents' needs:** Understand your parents' medical conditions and care needs to provide optimal support and anticipate future needs effectively.

- **Lean on your support system:** You don't have to do this alone. Consider who else can offer assistance and support, whether it is other family members, friends, or community resources. Building a solid support network will be invaluable on this journey.
- **Get things in order:** Before taking on the role of caregiver, it is essential to get your affairs in order. This includes sorting out any financial or logistical arrangements and ensuring you have access to essential documents and information related to your parents' care.
- **Acknowledge role reversal:** Recognize that becoming your parents' caregiver may significantly shift your relationship dynamic. Acknowledging your mixed emotions about this change and seeking support as you navigate this new chapter is okay.

Considering these factors before becoming your parents' caregiver will help ensure you are better prepared for the journey ahead. Remember, it is a role filled with challenges and opportunities for growth, connection, and love.

SIGNS YOU ARE ABOUT TO ENTER THE ROLE OF CAREGIVING

Are you noticing changes in your aging parents that suggest they might need more support? Many of us face this experience as our loved ones grow older. Whether it is subtle shifts in behavior or more obvious signs like difficulty with daily tasks, recognizing these indicators is the first step toward embracing the role of caregiving.

Let's explore some signs that indicate you're about to enter this important phase of life. Here is a list of what might be happening with your aging parents:

- **Bad breath or body odor:** Sometimes, these indicators can signal underlying health issues or changes in personal hygiene habits. It's essential to check in and address any concerns.
- **Personal hygiene:** Neglecting personal appearance or wearing dirty clothes may indicate difficulties with self-care and hygiene, necessitating support and encouragement.
- **Full bottles of prescription medications:** Ensuring your parents are managing their medications properly is crucial. Full bottles could suggest they are not taking their medications as prescribed, which requires attention.
- **Struggling to sit or stand independently:** Difficulty with mobility or muscle weakness might be behind this challenge. Discussing this with your aging parents can help identify solutions to enhance their independence and safety.
- **Unexplained bruises, scratches, or cuts:** These signs could point to accidents or falls, indicating a need for increased support or adjustments to the home environment to prevent further incidents.
- **Home looking different or unrecognizable:** Changes in their living space may signify difficulty maintaining or neglecting certain aspects of home care, prompting intervention.

- **Home maintenance issues:** Neglected household tasks or broken appliances pose safety risks and should be addressed promptly to maintain a safe living environment. Broken appliances may also indicate challenges in managing household responsibilities, necessitating support and intervention to maintain a safe and functional living environment.
- **Yard maintenance neglect:** Overgrown weeds or accumulating trash in the yard might indicate difficulty keeping up with outdoor chores, which warrants attention and support.
- **Changes in behavior, mood, or personality:** These changes could indicate various issues, including cognitive decline or mental health concerns, necessitating further assessment and support.
- **Changes in behavior toward others:** Shifts in their interactions with others may signal mental or emotional well-being changes that should be addressed and supported.
- **Spending less time outside the home:** Isolation can impact mental and physical well-being. Encouraging social engagement or participation in outdoor activities is crucial for their overall health.
- **Forgetting appointments:** Memory issues can be concerning and may require the implementation of strategies or tools to help them stay organized and on track with their appointments.
- **Changes in eating habits:** Poor nutrition can affect overall health, so ensuring access to nutritious meals is vital. Any significant changes in eating habits should be addressed and evaluated.

- **Progressive health conditions:** Declining health may necessitate exploring professional care options to ensure they receive the support and assistance they need.
- **Financial matters:** Late bill payments or calls from collection agencies could indicate challenges managing finances, requiring assistance or intervention to ensure financial stability.
- **Misplacing items:** Forgetfulness can be a sign of cognitive decline, so implementing strategies to help them stay organized and remember important items is essential.
- **Accidents or safety concerns:** Increased accidents or decreased focus on safety may indicate declining cognitive or physical abilities, requiring adjustments to ensure their safety at home.
- **Difficulty with daily tasks:** Struggling with chores or activities of daily living may indicate the need for assistance or modifications to their environment to enhance independence and safety.

These points can be challenging, but addressing concerns with compassion and support is essential. Remember, you are not alone in navigating these challenges.

GETTING STARTED AS YOUR PARENTS' CAREGIVER

Becoming your parents' caregiver is a journey filled with love, responsibility, and, yes, challenges. As you step into this role, it is essential to understand what it entails and how to get started. This section explores how to embark on your caregiving journey, beginning with understanding the role and your parents' needs.

What Is a Caregiver's Job?

Caregivers provide their aging parents physical, emotional, and sometimes financial support. Their role may include assisting with daily activities like:

- bathing
- dressing
- preparing meals
- managing medications
- coordinating medical appointments
- providing companionship

Additionally, caregivers often advocate for their parents, ensuring they receive the care and support they need to maintain their quality of life.

Understanding Your Parents' Needs

Before you can effectively care for your parents, you need to understand their needs. This involves open and honest communication about their current health, medical conditions, and any challenges they may face.

Take the time to listen to their concerns and preferences and involve them in decisions about their care whenever possible. By understanding their needs and preferences, you can provide personalized, compassionate care that enhances their well-being and maintains their dignity.

Communicating With Your Parents

Engage in open, empathetic conversations with your parents about their needs and preferences. Encourage your parents to share any concerns or challenges they may be experiencing and listen attentively to their perspectives.

Fostering clear communication can help you better understand your parents' needs and provide support tailored to their circumstances. Additionally, involving your parents in discussions about their care can empower them and help them feel more in control of their situation.

Assessing Physical and Emotional Well-Being

Observe your parents' physical and emotional state to identify areas where they need assistance or support. Pay attention to signs of physical decline, like difficulty with mobility or changes in appetite, and indicators of emotional distress, like increased irritability or withdrawal. By regularly assessing their well-being, you can proactively address any issues and ensure they receive the appropriate care and support.

By understanding the role of a caregiver and taking the time to communicate with your parents about their needs, you can lay a strong foundation for your caregiving journey. Remember that being a caregiver is a journey of learning and growth, and it's okay to seek support from others as you navigate this important role.

Getting Things in Order

Organizing is key to ensuring your parents' well-being and managing their affairs effectively when you become their caregiver. Organizing these details will streamline your caregiving responsibilities and provide peace of mind, knowing you are prepared to advocate effectively for your parents' needs. Remember, you're not alone in this journey; seeking professional or group support can provide valuable guidance and assistance.

Here's a personalized checklist to help you get things in order:

- **Bank accounts:** List all your parents' bank accounts, including checking, savings, and any other accounts they may have. This inventory will facilitate better financial management, ensuring timely bill payments and effective budgeting.
- **Insurance policies:** Collect information on your parents' health, life, and long-term care insurance policies. A comprehensive list of their coverage will aid in healthcare decision-making and access to necessary services.
- **Healthcare providers:** Create a list of your parents' regular healthcare providers, including primary care physicians, specialists, therapists, and other medical professionals they see regularly. This documentation will streamline communication and coordination of care between providers.

- **Diagnoses:** Track your parents' medical conditions, diagnoses, treatments, and therapies. Maintaining a record of their health history allows you to anticipate their healthcare needs and advocate for appropriate care when interacting with healthcare professionals.
- **Medications:** Compile a detailed list of your parents' medications, including the name of each medication, dosage, frequency, and prescribing physician. This medication list will help prevent errors and ensure healthcare providers have accurate information about your parents' prescriptions.
- **Directives:** Ensure you have copies of your parents' advance directives, such as living wills and healthcare power of attorney documents. These legal documents outline their preferences for medical treatment and appoint a healthcare proxy to make decisions on their behalf if they become incapacitated.
- **Finances:** Collect information about your parents' financial resources, including investments, assets, pensions, retirement accounts, Social Security benefits, and any additional sources of income. This financial inventory will provide a clear picture of their financial situation and help you make informed decisions about their financial management and long-term planning.

Dealing With Stubborn Parents

Conversing with your stubborn parents can be quite challenging, but it is essential to approach the situation with empathy, patience, and understanding. Taking the time to actively listen to your parents' concerns and validate their feelings can make a huge difference in finding common ground. Expressing your thoughts and feelings openly while maintaining a respectful tone is also helpful.

You and your parents can work toward a more harmonious relationship by encouraging an open and honest dialogue. Remember, change may not happen overnight, but with determination and compassion, progress is possible. Here is some advice to help you navigate this delicate process:

- **Initiate the conversation early:** Discuss important issues with your parents when everyone is calm and open to discussion.
- **Understand your parent's concerns and behaviors:** Take the time to understand your parents' perspectives, concerns, and the reasons behind their stubbornness. Empathize with their fears, insecurities, and desire to maintain independence, even if it conflicts with your wishes.
- **Evaluate your parent's current situation:** Assess your parents' physical and mental well-being and living arrangements to tailor your approach to their needs.
- **Start with the most important issues:** Prioritize critical issues affecting your parents' safety, health, and quality of life, such as medical care and financial planning.
- **Be calm but persistent:** Approach conversations calmly and advocate for your parents' well-being. Keep communication open and express concerns with empathy.

- **Treat your parents like adults:** Respect their independence, involve them in decision-making, and validate their feelings and concerns to show support.
- **Let them make their own decisions:** Empower your parents' independence by offering guidance and encouragement while respecting their autonomy. When situations are beyond your control, gracefully step back, trusting their judgment and offering unwavering support without imposing your own preferences.
- **Create a backup plan:** Create a plan if your parents' refusal to accept help becomes a barrier to their well-being. Identify alternative solutions or support.
- **Create a support system for your parents:** Create a support network that includes family, friends, and healthcare providers to assist and encourage your parents.
- **Be honest with how it affects you:** Be honest with your parents about how their stubbornness or resistance to help affects you. Express concerns with empathy.

MOURNING THE LOSS: PREPARING FOR THE ROLE REVERSAL

As we journey through life, we transition from being cared for by our parents to caring for them. This role reversal presents emotional and practical challenges.

As we grow, our parents age and become less capable, requiring our support. The shift from being a child to a caregiver is complex and emotional, involving practical care and emotional adjustments. This transition may bring feelings of loss, responsibility, and a redefinition of identity.

It's essential to seek support to navigate this transition successfully. It's also crucial for aging parents to receive the care they need. Understanding the challenges and seeking assistance can make this transition smoother for everyone involved. Here's some personal advice to help navigate this journey:

- **Set boundaries:** As a caregiver, clearly communicate with love and firmness. Remember, it's essential for your well-being. It's okay to say no or ask for help when needed.
- **Mourn the loss of traditional roles:** Mourning traditional roles is natural. Embrace emotions, talk with friends or a therapist, and give yourself time to adjust. It's okay to mourn while finding deeper connection and growth.
- **Keep lines of communication open:** Open communication is crucial in role reversal. Talk openly about needs, preferences, and concerns. Listen attentively, validate feelings, and express thoughts without judgment. Foster mutual respect and understanding for a stronger bond.
- **Seek support:** You don't have to go it alone. Seek support from family, friends, or professionals. Sharing experiences and seeking advice is empowering; seeking help is a sign of strength.

- **Take care of yourself:** As you care for your parents, prioritize self-care. Engage in activities that nourish your body and mind. Remember, you can't pour from an empty cup. Take care of yourself first.
- **Adapt and be flexible:** The caregiving journey is dynamic and requires flexibility and patience. Embrace each moment, stay present, and celebrate small victories. Navigate role reversal with grace, compassion, and love.

SURVIVAL TIPS

Surviving and thriving as a caregiver requires incredible resilience, ongoing self-care, and a robust and supportive network. It is a journey filled with challenges and moments of profound connection and fulfillment. Taking time for yourself, seeking support from others, and finding joy in the small victories are all essential parts of this vital role. Remember, you are not alone on this journey. Here are some personal tips to help you navigate this challenging time:

- **Ask for help:** Asking for help isn't a weakness; it shows strength and self-awareness. Seek assistance from family, friends, or caregivers.
- **Maintain good habits:** Prioritize your well-being with healthy habits. Self-care is crucial for your health and can enable better care for aging parents.
- **Modify the home:** Ensure a safe, comfortable home for aging parents by modifying the environment with grab bars, decluttering, and improving accessibility.

- **Get plenty of rest:** Prioritize sleep to recharge. Lack of sleep impairs cognitive function and mood. Establish a bedtime routine and delegate caregiving.
- **Stay socially active:** Stay connected with friends, family, and community groups to reduce isolation and maintain mental health. Schedule regular outings and calls.
- **Join a support group:** Connect with other caregivers for advice and support. Peer support can provide validation, reassurance, and camaraderie in caregiving.

Remember, caregiving is a journey filled with both challenges and rewards. By prioritizing self-care, seeking support, and practicing resilience, you can survive and thrive as a caregiver, maintaining your well-being while providing compassionate care to your loved one.

In this chapter, we explored some crucial survival tips for caregivers, each tailored to help you endure and thrive in your role. We discovered the importance of asking for help, maintaining healthy habits, creating a supportive home environment, prioritizing rest, staying socially active, and finding solace in support groups. These tips aren't just abstract concepts but actionable steps designed to empower you in your caregiving journey.

In the next chapter, we will dive deeper into the practical aspects of caregiving by exploring strategies to organize and streamline life at home. From managing medications to coordinating appointments and ensuring a safe living environment, Chapter 2 equips you with the tools and insights to navigate the daily challenges of caregiving confidently and efficiently.

So, let's embark on this next chapter together, ready to discover new ways to enhance your caregiving experience and create a supportive home environment where your aging parents and you can thrive. Get ready to roll up your sleeves and dive into the heart of caregiving!

ORGANIZE LIFE AT HOME

Accepting the rapid decline in your parents' physical health can be emotionally daunting. This reality hit Sam and me during our first private conversation about our new caregiver roles. With Mike's family history of dementia in mind, we agreed that they needed to remain in a familiar and comfortable setting.

We believed adjusting to a new living arrangement would be far more disruptive for them than us. Given the physical decline and the anticipated short-term memory issues, we understood that falls might become more frequent over time. To avoid adding confusion and disorientation, we moved into Mike and Kay's home rather than relocating them to a new environment. Mike and Kay, ever gracious and generous, insisted we take the main suite, treating us as guests in their own home and wanting to show their appreciation for our commitment to care for them. We appreciated their thoughtfulness but also understood that having them stay where they were most familiar with their bedtime routine would be most helpful moving forward.

At this stage, they could still foresee potential future challenges and, after much discussion and convincing, agreed that staying in their familiar surroundings was the best option. Although no immediate changes were made, we suggested practical improvements to enhance their safety, like installing handrails near the bathroom facilities. Initially, Mike and Kay were hesitant, but as falls became more frequent, they saw the value and agreed to these modifications.

GETTING HOME LIFE IN ORDER

Organizing your living environment for your aging parents involves more than just tidying up or rearranging furniture. It is about creating a living space that caters to their evolving needs and prioritizes safety, comfort, and accessibility. This process requires thoughtful planning and implementing various modifications and adjustments to ensure your home is conducive to their well-being.

Arranging your home for your aging parents encompasses a range of tasks, from decluttering and streamlining to installing safety features and incorporating assistive technology. These tasks are all intended to create a supportive environment that promotes independence and enhances their quality of life. It is about ensuring that every aspect of your home—from room layout to everyday items—is tailored to meet their needs and preferences.

This section will explore the importance of organizing your home for your aging parents. You will delve into practical tips and strategies for creating a safe, comfortable. A functional living space that empowers them to age in place with dignity and confidence.

Whether making minor adjustments or undertaking more significant renovations, the goal remains to ensure your home is a welcoming and secure haven where your aging parents can thrive.

So, let's dive in and discover how you can transform your home into a supportive environment that meets your aging loved ones' unique needs. This will allow them to continue living independently and enjoying the comforts of home for years to come.

CREATING A SAFE LIVING ENVIRONMENT

Creating a safe living environment for aging parents is crucial as they navigate their golden years. Their changing mobility and sensory abilities make them more vulnerable to accidents. Proactively addressing potential hazards at home can significantly reduce the risk of falls and injuries, allowing them to maintain independence and quality of life.

Walk around their home to look for anything that could threaten their safety, such as loose rugs, electrical cords, slippery floors, or poorly lit areas. Identifying these hazards early on empowers you to take action and make necessary adjustments to create a safer living environment.

Next up, let's explore different home modifications that can ensure safety. Here is a breakdown into specific areas of the house to cover all bases:

- **Entrance and exits:** Ensure clear pathways for easy movement, install handrails for stability, and provide sufficient lighting for visibility, especially at night
- **Living room:** Arrange furniture to create wide pathways and minimize tripping hazards. Use nonslip rugs or secure them with double-sided tape to prevent slipping. Install sturdy handrails or grab bars near seating areas for additional support.
- **Bedroom:** Opt for a main-floor bedroom for easier access. Ensure the bed is at a suitable height for easy entry and exit, and install bedside lighting and reachable storage for added convenience.
- **Bathroom:** Install grab bars near the toilet and in the shower or bathtub. Use non-slip mats to prevent falls, and consider adding a raised toilet seat or shower bench for added comfort and safety.
- **Kitchen:** Organize kitchen items within reach to minimize stretching or bending. Install lever-style faucet handles for easier use, and ensure adequate lighting over work areas for improved visibility.
- **Hallways and staircases:** Keep hallways clutter-free and well-lit to prevent tripping. Install handrails on both sides of staircases for support and safety, and consider adding stairlifts or ramps for more effortless mobility if necessary.
- **Storage areas:** Store frequently used items at waist level to minimize bending or reaching. Label storage containers and shelves for easy identification, and

ensure clear pathways and adequate lighting in storage areas.

- **Emergency contacts and supplies:** Keep emergency contact information easily accessible. Install smoke and carbon monoxide detectors throughout the house, and consider a medical alert system for added peace of mind in emergencies.

By implementing these simple yet effective modifications, we can significantly enhance the safety and well-being of our aging parents at home. Remember, every minor adjustment creates a safer and more comfortable environment for our loved ones.

SAFEGUARDING YOUR AGING PARENTS' WELL-BEING

Falls are a common concern for older adults and can have serious consequences. Understanding the causes of falls and taking proactive steps to prevent them is essential for maintaining your aging parents' safety and well-being. Let's explore why falls happen, practical measures to avoid them, and what to do if an accident occurs.

What Causes Falls in Older Adults?

Understanding the many factors contributing to falls in older adults is crucial for effective prevention strategies. The risk of falls can stem from various sources, from physical decline due to age-related changes to medication side effects and environmental hazards. Chronic health conditions and a lack of exercise further exacerbate these risks, highlighting the importance of proactive measures to ensure the safety and well-being of older adults. Several factors contribute to falls in older adults, including:

- **Physical decline:** Age-related changes in vision, balance, and muscle strength can significantly increase the risk of falls among older adults. As individuals age, their vision may deteriorate, making it harder to navigate their surroundings safely. Additionally, balance and muscle strength changes can affect stability, increasing the likelihood of falls, especially when performing daily activities such as walking or standing.
- **Medication side effects:** Certain medications prescribed to manage various health conditions can have side effects that increase the risk of falls. Medications such as sedatives, antidepressants, and antihypertensives can cause dizziness, drowsiness, or impaired coordination, making individuals more susceptible to falls, particularly if they are taking multiple medications or experiencing dosage changes.
- **Environmental hazards:** Environmental factors significantly affect fall risk among older adults. Cluttered walkways, poor lighting, slippery floors, and uneven surfaces in the home or community settings can pose significant hazards and increase the likelihood of falls. Addressing these environmental hazards through home modifications and improving safety features can help reduce fall risk and enhance overall safety.

- **Chronic health conditions:** Chronic health conditions such as arthritis, Parkinson's disease, and diabetes can affect mobility, balance, and coordination, increasing the risk of falls. Individuals with these conditions may experience muscle weakness, joint stiffness, or gait disturbances that compromise their ability to move safely and maintain balance. Managing these underlying health conditions through appropriate treatment and rehabilitation can help reduce fall risk and improve overall health outcomes.

- **Lack of exercise:** Sedentary lifestyles and lack of physical activity contribute to muscle weakness, reduced balance, and impaired mobility, increasing the risk of falls among older adults. Regular exercise and physical activity are essential for maintaining strength, flexibility, and balance, which are crucial for preventing falls and promoting overall health and well-being. Walking, strength training, and balance exercises can help older adults improve their physical fitness and reduce fall risk.

Preventing Falls: Steps to Take

Taking proactive steps is essential when safeguarding your aging parent against the risk of falls. By enforcing preventive measures, you can significantly reduce the likelihood of accidents and promote their safety and well-being. Each action is vital in fall prevention, from making home safety modifications to encouraging regular exercise and medication management. This section will explore key strategies and steps to help create a safer environment and minimize the risk of falls for your loved one.

To reduce the risk of falls for your aging parent, consider the following preventive measures:

- **Home safety modifications:** Remove tripping hazards, improve lighting, install grab bars and handrails, and make other modifications to create a safer home environment.
- **Regular exercise:** Encourage your parents to participate in activities that improve strength, balance, and flexibility, such as walking, tai chi, or yoga.
- **Medication management:** Review your parents' medications with their healthcare provider to identify any that may increase fall risk and explore alternative options if necessary.
- **Regular vision and hearing checks:** Ensure your parents' vision and hearing are regularly evaluated and address any issues affecting their ability to navigate their environment safely.
- **Footwear:** Encourage your parents to wear supportive, nonslip footwear with proper traction to reduce the risk of slipping and falling.
- **Assistive devices:** If your parents use mobility aids such as canes or walkers, ensure they are properly fitted and in good condition.
- **Fall detection devices:** Consider investing in a device or pendant that can automatically alert caregivers or emergency services if a fall occurs.

What to Do if Your Aging Parents Fall

Despite our best efforts to prevent them, falls can still happen to our aging parents, and knowing how to respond effectively is crucial for their safety and well-being. This section will explore important steps if your parents experience a fall. From assessing for injuries and offering immediate support to addressing the cause of the fall and seeking medical attention, each action plays a vital role in ensuring the best possible outcome for your loved one. Being prepared and proactive can help safeguard your aging parents' health and independence in the event of a fall.

If your aging parent experiences a fall, take the following steps:

1. **Assess for injuries:** Check your parent for any signs of injury, such as bruises, cuts, or fractures, and seek medical attention if necessary.
2. **Offer support:** Help your parent safely get up from the floor or assist them in moving to a comfortable position if injured.
3. **Evaluate the cause:** Determine what caused the fall and address any environmental hazards or underlying health issues to prevent future incidents.
4. **Seek medical attention:** If your parent experiences pain, dizziness, or other symptoms after a fall, consult their healthcare provider for further evaluation and treatment.

Taking proactive steps to prevent falls and knowing how to respond if an accident occurs can help safeguard your aging parents' well-being and promote their independence and quality of life.

TECHNOLOGY AND YOUR AGING PARENTS

Technology has the power to revolutionize daily tasks and bolster safety for aging parents, significantly enhancing their quality of life. With a range of tailored solutions, such as health monitoring devices and smart home systems, we can cater to the specific needs of older individuals. Wearable health trackers and emergency response systems offer peace of mind for both seniors and their families.

Moreover, smart home devices like automated lighting and voice-activated assistants streamline daily living for seniors. Embracing these advancements positively impacts the well-being of our aging loved ones, ensuring safety, security, and improved communication. Let's explore how integrating technology into their daily lives can empower seniors to live independently and with greater peace of mind.

Importance of Technology for Making Life Easier for Aging Parents

As our loved ones age, integrating technology into their daily lives can significantly enhance their quality of life and overall well-being. Technology offers many benefits for aging parents, from ensuring safety and security to facilitating communication and assisting with daily tasks. In this section, we'll delve into the importance of technology in making life easier for seniors.

From enhanced safety features like medical alert systems and fall detection sensors to improved communication through smartphones and video calling apps, we'll explore how these innovations can empower seniors to live independently and with greater peace of mind.

Additionally, we'll discuss how technology aids medication management, assists with daily tasks, and facilitates proactive health monitoring, ultimately promoting a healthier, more connected lifestyle for aging parents.

Technology offers numerous benefits for aging parents, including:

- **Enhanced safety:** Medical alert systems, fall detection sensors, and home monitoring cameras provide peace of mind and prompt emergency assistance.
- **Improved communication:** Smartphones, tablets, and video calling apps enable easy and accessible communication with family, friends, and healthcare providers, reducing social isolation and promoting connectedness.
- **Medication management:** Smart pill dispensers and reminder apps help seniors stay on track with their medication schedules, reducing the risk of missed doses or medication errors.
- **Assistance with daily tasks:** Smart home devices, voice assistants, and home automation systems can assist with tasks like turning on lights, adjusting thermostats, or setting reminders, making daily life more manageable.

- **Health monitoring:** Wearable fitness trackers, blood pressure monitors, and remote health monitoring devices allow seniors to track their health metrics and share data with healthcare providers to manage chronic conditions proactively.

Several devices are specifically designed to meet the needs of aging parents:

- **Medical alert systems:** These wearable devices allow seniors to call for emergency help with a button, connecting them to a monitoring center or designated caregivers.
- **Fall detection sensors:** Fall detection devices automatically detect falls and alert caregivers or emergency services, providing timely assistance in the event of an accident.
- **Smartphones and tablets:** These devices offer intuitive interfaces, large displays, and accessibility features tailored to seniors' needs, facilitating communication, entertainment, and access to information.
- **Smart home devices:** Smart thermostats, lighting systems, door locks, and security cameras can be controlled remotely or through voice commands, enhancing convenience and safety at home.
- **Medication reminder devices:** Smart pill dispensers, medication reminder apps, and electronic pillboxes help seniors manage their medication schedules and ensure they take the right pills at the right time.

- **Wearable health trackers:** Fitness trackers, smartwatches, and health monitoring devices allow seniors to monitor their activity levels, heart rate, sleep patterns, and other health metrics, promoting an active and healthy lifestyle.

By leveraging the power of technology and incorporating these devices into their daily lives, aging parents can enjoy greater independence, safety, and peace of mind. At the same time, caregivers can rest assured knowing their loved ones are well-supported and connected.

MONITORING AND ALERT SYSTEMS

Monitoring and alert systems are indispensable in caring for our aging parents, especially when physical presence isn't always feasible. These systems offer continuous surveillance and prompt alerts, providing caregivers with crucial support and peace of mind. Let's delve deeper into the benefits and considerations of these systems:

- **Emergency alerts:** In emergencies like falls or sudden health issues, alert systems swiftly notify caregivers or emergency services. This rapid response can significantly reduce the severity of injuries or complications by ensuring timely assistance and intervention.
- **Peace of mind:** Knowing that a monitoring system is actively safeguarding their parents reassures caregivers and reduces anxiety. Even when physical presence isn't possible, caregivers can trust that their

parents are being watched and that help will be alerted if needed.

- **Remote access:** Many monitoring systems offer remote access via smartphones or computers, enabling caregivers to monitor their parents' well-being from anywhere. This flexibility allows caregivers to stay informed and promptly address concerns, even when away from home.
- **Customizable features:** Monitoring systems often come with customizable features, allowing caregivers to tailor them to specific needs and preferences. These features accommodate individual requirements, from monitoring specific areas to setting alerts and adjusting settings.

What to Look for in an Elderly Monitoring System

- **Ease of use:** Ensure the system is user-friendly and intuitive so your parents can operate independently.
- **Features:** Based on your parents' needs, consider essential features like fall detection, emergency buttons, motion sensors, and video monitoring.
- **Reliability:** Opt for a system with a proven track record of accuracy and reliability in detecting and alerting to potential risks or emergencies.
- **Cost:** Evaluate the cost, including monthly fees or subscription plans, to ensure it fits your budget without compromising quality or features.
- **Compatibility:** Ensure the system is compatible with your parents' devices and home environment, including smartphones, tablets, and home automation systems.

Best Senior Monitoring Systems for Aging in Place

- **Medical alert systems:** Offer wearable devices with emergency buttons for 24-7 monitoring and support.
- **Smart home security systems:** Provide customizable features like motion sensors and video monitoring for comprehensive home security.
- **Smart wearables:** Offer health monitoring features like fall detection and GPS tracking for valuable insights into health and well-being.
- **Home automation systems:** Allow for remote monitoring and control of various home aspects, integrating with other devices for a comprehensive solution.

Monitoring Elderly Parents Remotely

Modern monitoring systems can help you remotely monitor your parents' safety and well-being using smartphone apps and cloud-based platforms. With real-time alerts, live video feeds, and the ability to control home settings remotely, you can ensure your parents' safety from anywhere.

By investing in a reliable home monitoring and alert system, you can give your parents the essential support they need, enabling them to age in place safely and independently. This offers peace of mind to the entire family.

This chapter explored ways to ensure a safe and supportive living environment for aging parents. From understanding the importance of safety measures to implementing home modifications and utilizing technology, we've covered ways to enhance their well-being and independence. As a caregiver, you can create a nurturing environment that promotes safety and peace of mind by taking proactive steps to prevent falls, monitoring their health, and embracing assistive gadgets.

As we journey through the intricacies of caregiving, our next destination awaits in Chapter 3: "Navigate Legal and Financial Considerations." We'll delve into the critical aspects of managing legal matters and financial affairs to safeguard the interests of aging parents and caregivers alike. Get ready to explore essential guidance and practical tips to navigate this crucial aspect of caregiving with confidence and clarity.

NAVIGATE LEGAL AND FINANCIAL CONSIDERATIONS

M ike and Kay were always meticulous planners, ensuring they were prepared for emergencies with a fund set aside for unforeseen medical costs or urgent transportation needs in case of an accident or death. During their travels, they consistently showed us where they stored all important documents, including this emergency fund.

Discussing the potential need for access to these documents was uncomfortable, but we appreciated their foresight, especially when organizing the legal paperwork for our caregiving duties. Their will was already in place, so we reviewed and updated it, discussed any new preferences, and confirmed that Mike and Kay were fully competent when making these decisions. Sam's siblings were informed about their parents' wishes, and everyone agreed to honor these plans when necessary.

LEGAL CONSIDERATIONS FOR FAMILY CAREGIVERS

Understanding the legal and financial implications is crucial to caring for aging parents. These essential aspects will better equip you to ensure their well-being and security. This section will guide you through estate planning, healthcare directives, financial management, and long-term care options. With this practical advice, you'll be empowered to navigate this complex terrain confidently.

Family caregivers are vital for our aging loved ones' well-being. Legal matters can be daunting, but fear not! We're delving into the world of caregiver legalities. From knowing your rights to making crucial decisions, we're here to guide you. Join us as we demystify the power of attorney, healthcare directives, and elder law. Grab your legal compass, and let's navigate together! We'll ensure your loved ones receive the care they deserve while mastering the legal terrain.

The Right Documents

When it comes to your aging parents' legal and financial matters, having the proper documents in place is essential. These documents serve as a road map, guiding you through the complexities of estate planning, healthcare decisions, and financial management. Some key documents every caregiver should ensure are in order include:

- **Power of attorney (POA):** A POA allows someone to make legal and financial decisions for an incapacitated parent. Both types are essential.

- **Will or trust:** Your parents' will or trust outlines asset distribution after passing. Update it regularly to reflect changes in wishes or circumstances.
- **Advance directive:** An advance directive, known as a living will, specifies your parents' medical treatment and end-of-life care wishes.
- **HIPAA authorization:** This document allows healthcare providers to share your parents' medical information, enabling informed decisions about their care.
- **Financial account information:** Ensure you can access your parents' bank, investment, and retirement accounts to manage their finances and bills.
- **Insurance policies:** Monitor your parents' health, life, and long-term care insurance to manage healthcare costs and ensure entitlement benefits.
- **Property deeds and titles:** Ensure your parents' property and vehicle titles are in order and accessible to simplify future ownership transfers.

With these documents in place, you can better handle the legal and financial aspects of caring for your aging parents. Discuss these matters with your parents and other family members and consult with legal and financial professionals to ensure their wishes are respected and their interests are protected.

Make a Family Plan

Creating a family plan for managing the care of aging parents is a proactive and collaborative approach to ensure their well-being and address their evolving needs. Here's how to formulate a comprehensive family plan:

- **Initiate family discussions:** Schedule a family meeting to discuss your parents' needs and roles and encourage open communication and active participation from everyone.
- **Identify key decision-makers:** Decide who will make your parents' healthcare, financial, and legal decisions by appointing a caregiver and power of attorney.
- **Assess resources and support:** Assess family resources like time, skills, and finances. Identify needs for professional caregiving, financial planning, or legal assistance.
- **Compile important documents:** Organize wills, insurance, financial info, and property deeds. Ensure easy access for relevant family members.
- **Develop a care plan:** Develop a care plan for your parents' medical, social, and emotional needs, including healthcare preferences, daily living assistance, and social activities.
- **Establish communication channels:** Update the family on the parents' condition and care plan through regular communication, such as meetings, email, or a shared platform.
- **Delegate responsibilities:** Assign family responsibilities based on skills, availability, and preferences, such as medical coordination, finances, transportation, or respite care.
- **Create contingency plans:** Create contingency plans that anticipate challenges and develop plans.

- **Review and revise regularly:** Update the family plan regularly as your parents' needs change. Schedule family meetings to discuss any adjustments or updates.
- **Seek professional guidance:** Don't hesitate to consult legal, financial, and healthcare professionals for valuable expertise and guidance in complex matters.

By creating a family plan that addresses the holistic needs of your aging parents and fosters collaboration among family members, you can ensure that they receive the support and care they deserve while minimizing stress and uncertainty for everyone involved.

Organize Important Papers

Organizing essential papers is a crucial step in preparing for the care of aging parents. Here's a systematic approach to help you get started:

- **Gather documents:** Collect all relevant documents in one central location. This includes legal, financial, medical, and personal records. Retrieve items such as:

  - birth certificates
  - Social Security cards
  - marriage certificates
  - wills and trusts
  - power of attorney documents
  - advance directives (living wills)

- insurance policies
- bank statements
- investment account information
- property deeds
- vehicle titles
- medical records
- prescription medication lists
- contact information for healthcare providers
- funeral or burial instructions

- **Sort and categorize:** Organize the documents into categories for easy reference. Consider using labeled folders, binders, or a filing cabinet. Common categories may include:

  - personal identification
  - legal documents
  - financial records
  - medical information
  - insurance policies
  - property and asset documents
  - end-of-life preferences

- **Create a master list:** List all documents, including name, location, and contact info, for quick family reference.
- **Secure storage:** For accessibility and security, store important documents in a secure location, such as a fireproof safe, filing cabinet, or digital storage.
- **Make copies:** Make copies of important documents and store them separately. Secure digital copies on a password-protected device.

- **Update regularly:** Update documents to reflect changes in your parents' circumstances or preferences. Review annually and make necessary revisions.
- **Communicate with family:** Inform family about important document locations. Ensure designated individuals understand their roles in document management and decision-making.
- **Consider professional assistance:** Seek professional advice for managing essential documents to ensure they're organized properly for your specific needs.

By organizing important papers in a systematic and accessible manner, you can ensure that you and your family are prepared to manage your aging parents' affairs effectively and provide them with the care and support they need.

Tax Breaks and Life Insurance Deals

When caring for aging parents, exploring potential tax breaks and life insurance deals that could help alleviate financial burdens and provide additional support is essential. Here are some avenues to consider:

Tax Breaks

- **Medical expenses deduction:** Deduct medical expenses for aging parents, such as healthcare premiums, long-term care costs, and home modifications, to reduce taxable income.

- **Dependent care credit:** Care expenses for working and aging parents may qualify for a Dependent Care Credit covering adult day care and in-home care.
- **Flexible spending accounts (FSAs) and health savings accounts (HSAs):** FSAs and HSAs can pay for aging parents' medical expenses pre-tax, reducing your taxable income.

Life Insurance Deals

- **Long-term care insurance:** Long-term care insurance covers nursing homes, assisted living, and in-home care. Premiums may be tax-deductible, and benefits may be tax-free.
- **Life insurance with living benefits:** Some life insurance policies allow policyholders to access a portion of the death benefit for medical or long-term care costs.

Consult with a financial advisor: A financial advisor offers personalized advice on tax-efficient strategies, life insurance, and maximizing available benefits.

Research government programs: Find government programs that offer financial help for caregivers, including Medicaid waivers, tax credits, and state-specific long-term care support.

Review employer benefits: Check if your employer offers caregiver support, such as flexible work arrangements, assistance programs, or discounted insurance.

By proactively seeking out tax breaks and life insurance deals, you can potentially reduce financial stress and ensure you have the resources to provide quality care for your aging parents. Consult with financial professionals and explore all available options to make informed decisions that best meet your family's needs.

ASSISTING WITH ESTATE PLANNING

Embarking on estate planning for your elderly parent is a journey of meaningful conversations and safeguarding your family's future. It's about preserving your parents' legacy, protecting their assets, and ensuring their wishes are honored. In this guide, we'll navigate estate planning together, crafting wills and trusts and exploring creative ways to pass on family heirlooms.

Let's transform this daunting task into a fulfilling and meaningful experience for your entire family. Please grab a cup of coffee, pull up a chair, and embark on this empowering journey to give your parents the peace of mind they deserve.

Will

A will is a legal document that outlines a person's wishes regarding the distribution of their assets and the care of their dependents after death. It allows individuals to specify how they want their property, belongings, and finances divided among their heirs or beneficiaries. Having a will is essential because it provides clarity and guidance to loved ones, ensures that assets are distributed according to the individual's wishes, and can help prevent disputes among family members.

Additionally, a will allows individuals to designate guardians for minor children and appoint executors to fulfill their wishes. Overall, a will is a critical tool for estate planning that helps provide peace of mind and security for the individual and their family.

Power of Attorney

A power of attorney (POA) is a legal document that grants someone else the authority to act on your behalf in various legal and financial matters. The person granting the authority is known as the "principal," while the individual receiving the authority is referred to as the "agent" or "attorney-in-fact." There are different types of power of attorney, each serving specific purposes:

- **General power of attorney:** This document grants the agent the power to temporarily manage legal/financial affairs on the principal's behalf or due to illness or travel.
- **Durable power of attorney:** A durable power of attorney remains effective even if the principal becomes incapacitated, providing continuity of decision-making.
- **Limited or special power of attorney:** This document grants the agent powers to perform specific tasks or transactions on behalf of the principal, such as real estate or financial management, during absence.

- **Healthcare power of attorney:** Also known as a healthcare proxy or medical power of attorney, this document appoints an agent to make healthcare decisions on behalf of the principal if the principal becomes incapacitated and unable to communicate their wishes.

Having a power of attorney is crucial for ensuring that someone you trust can manage your affairs and make decisions on your behalf if you cannot do so yourself. It provides peace of mind and allows for seamless decision-making in times of need. However, it's important to carefully consider who you appoint as your agent and clearly outline the scope of their authority in the document. Consulting with a legal professional can help ensure that your power of attorney meets your needs and complies with relevant laws and regulations.

Advance Derivatives

Advance directives are legal documents that allow individuals to specify their preferences for medical treatment and end-of-life care if they cannot communicate their wishes. These documents guide healthcare providers and family members regarding the type of care the individual desires.

There are two main types of advance directives:

- **Living will:** A living will outlines medical treatment preferences for life-sustaining measures, resuscitation, and artificial nutrition in case of incapacity.

- **Healthcare power of attorney:** A healthcare proxy appoints an agent to make medical decisions based on the individual's wishes if the individual cannot communicate.

Advance directives ensure medical treatment preferences are honored. Outlining end-of-life care preferences in advance relieves loved ones of difficult choices. Discuss with family and healthcare providers and keep them updated to reflect preferences and values accurately.

Trusts

Trusts can be valuable estate planning tools for aging parents, providing a way to manage and distribute assets while addressing specific needs and concerns. Here's what you need to know about trusts for aging parents:

Definition: Trusts are legal agreements where a trustee manages assets for a beneficiary. They can be living or testamentary.

Types of Trusts

- **Revocable living trust:** A revocable trust allows control of assets until death when they are transferred to beneficiaries without probate.
- **Irrevocable trust:** The grantor cannot change an irrevocable trust, which offers asset protection and tax benefits but also causes the grantor to lose control.

- **Special needs trust:** Designed to provide financial support for individuals with disabilities or special needs, a special needs trust allows the beneficiary to receive supplemental assistance without jeopardizing eligibility for government benefits.
- **Asset protection trust:** This type of trust is designed to shield assets from creditors and lawsuits, protecting the grantor's wealth.
- **Charitable trust:** Charitable trust lets donors donate assets while retaining benefits like tax deductions or receiving income during their lifetime.

Benefits of Trusts for Aging Parents

- **Asset management:** Trusts enable aging parents to appoint a trustee to manage their assets if they become incapacitated or unable to handle their finances.
- **Probate avoidance:** Assets held in a trust can bypass the probate process, saving time and expenses associated with probate administration.
- **Privacy:** Trusts offer greater privacy than wills, as trust documents are not publicly disclosed during probate.
- **Control over distribution:** Trusts allow parents to specify how and when assets should be distributed to beneficiaries, providing flexibility and control over their estate plan.
- **Protection:** Certain types of trusts, such as irrevocable trusts and asset protection trusts, can offer protection against creditors, lawsuits, and long-term care costs.

Considerations

- **Legal and tax implications:** Consult an estate planning attorney to ensure tax and legal compliance when building a trust.
- **Costs:** Consider the trust's costs before creation, including upfront and ongoing fees.
- **Family dynamics:** Clear trust guidance and open communication prevent family conflicts.

Trusts can be valuable tools for aging parents to manage and protect their assets, provide for their loved ones, and achieve their estate planning goals. By understanding the types of trusts available and seeking professional guidance, parents can create a comprehensive estate plan that meets their needs and ensures their legacy is preserved for future generations.

Reducing Estate Taxes

Many individuals seek to reduce estate taxes as they plan their estates to minimize the tax burden on their heirs and preserve more of their assets for future generations.

Working with a qualified estate planning attorney or financial advisor is essential to develop a comprehensive estate plan that considers your unique financial situation, goals, and tax implications. By implementing strategic planning techniques, you can minimize estate taxes and preserve more assets for your heirs and beneficiaries. Here are some strategies to consider for reducing estate taxes:

Probate

Probate is the legal process through which a deceased person's assets are distributed to their heirs or beneficiaries, and their debts are paid off. The court supervises the probate process and ensures that the deceased person's final wishes, as outlined in their will (if they have one), are fulfilled.

Here's an overview of the probate process:

1. **Initiating probate:** One files a petition with the probate court to initiate probate. A valid will is submitted with the petition. Without it, an administrator is appointed.
2. **Appointing an executor/administrator:** The court appoints an executor or administrator to manage the estate. They inventory assets, notify creditors and beneficiaries, pay debts and taxes, and distribute assets according to the will or state law.
3. **Notifying creditors and beneficiaries:** The executor must notify creditors and publish in a local newspaper to alert unknown creditors. Creditors have several months to file claims for outstanding debts.
4. **Distributing of assets:** After paying debts and taxes, assets are divided among beneficiaries by will or state law. Court approval is necessary, and a final report must be submitted.
5. **Closing the estate:** Once all debts have been paid and assets distributed, the executor/administrator petitions the court to close the estate. If satisfied, the

court reviews the final accounting and issues an order closing the probate process.

Probate laws and procedures vary by state, and the process can be complex based on factors like estate size and disputes. Estate planning strategies, such as a living trust, can decrease the probate process. An experienced estate planning attorney can help navigate probate and ensure final wishes are carried out.

Legal Help

End-of-life planning is a crucial aspect of elder care, and seeking legal help from an elder care attorney can provide valuable assistance to family caregivers. Here's how an elder care attorney can help you:

- **Navigating complex legal issues:** An elder care attorney can assist with end-of-life planning, wills, trusts, advance directives, and healthcare decisions.
- **Drafting estate planning documents:** An elder care attorney can help create estate planning documents to document your loved one's wishes and prevent disputes legally.
- **Maximizing benefits and protections:** Elder care attorneys assist with navigating Medicaid, Social Security, and asset protection to maximize benefits and prevent depletion.
- **Addressing capacity and guardianship issues:** If your elderly loved ones are experiencing cognitive decline, consult an elder care attorney to establish guardianship or conservatorship for their protection.

- **Mediating and resolving disputes:** When family members disagree on end-of-life care or estate planning decisions, an elder care attorney can serve as a neutral mediator to facilitate communication and resolve conflicts. They can help find common ground and develop solutions that meet the needs and preferences of all parties involved.
- **Staying current on legal changes:** Laws and regulations on end-of-life planning and elder care constantly evolve. An elder care attorney stays abreast of these changes and can advise you on any updates or modifications to your loved one's estate plan or advance directives.

Overall, an elder care attorney is vital in helping family caregivers navigate the complex legal landscape of end-of-life planning. By seeking legal guidance, caregivers can ensure that their loved ones' wishes are honored, their assets are protected, and their best interests are served during this challenging time.

FINANCIAL CONSIDERATIONS

Consolidating accounts and credit cards, setting up automatic bill payments, and managing your aging parents' finances effectively are essential aspects of caregiving that can help ensure their financial well-being. Here's more information on each of these tasks:

- **Consolidate accounts and credit cards:** To avoid missed payments or oversights, simplify money management by consolidating your parents' financial accounts and credit cards.
- **Set up automatic bill payments:** Automate recurring payments to avoid late fees. Set up automatic payments with parents for essential expenses.
- **Eliminate duplicate or unused services and subscriptions:** Cancel unnecessary subscriptions to reduce spending and free up funds.
- **Audit your parents' wallets:** Regularly review parents' wallets to minimize identity theft and financial fraud. Organize essential cards and documents.
- **Limit spending:** Encourage parents to budget and limit non-essential spending to achieve financial goals.
- **Don't co-mingle your parents' finances with yours:** Separate personal and business finances to avoid legal issues and complications with taxes, estate planning, and financial management.
- **Know how to monitor your parents' finances:** Regularly monitor your parents' finances using apps to detect irregularities and unauthorized activity.
- **Keep good records:** Organize your parents' financial documents, including bank statements and insurance policies, for easy access when needed.
- **Plan:** With your parents, plan for future expenses and emergencies. Create a comprehensive financial plan that anticipates potential challenges.

By implementing these strategies and actively managing your aging parents' finances, you can help ensure their financial security and well-being as they age. Open communication, collaboration, and regular monitoring are essential to effective financial caregiving and promoting peace of mind for you and your parents.

Chapter 3 highlighted managing and safeguarding aging parents' finances. Strategies included consolidating accounts, setting up automatic bill payments, and limiting spending for financial well-being and security.

Moving on to Chapter 4, "Caring for Your Parents' Physical Health," we'll cover managing chronic conditions and medication regimens, promoting healthy lifestyle choices, and addressing mobility challenges.

4

CARING FOR YOUR PARENTS' PHYSICAL HEALTH

Mike and Kay maintained good health throughout their lives, only visiting doctors for serious illnesses or injuries. In her 50s, Kay was diagnosed with type I diabetes. As a nurse, she was adept at handling most medical issues and seldom sought doctor's visits, embodying the typical nurse's reluctance to be patients themselves.

She even removed a deep splinter from Sam using a needle and tweezers. On another occasion, when Mike was writhing in pain on the bathroom floor, thinking he was experiencing a severe internal issue, Kay diagnosed him with a kidney stone. She reassured him that the pain would subside once the stone passed.

Getting Mike and Kay to commit to regular medical checkups required us to mark the appointments on the calendar well in advance, helping them mentally prepare and accept the need for these visits. The calendar later proved helpful in tracking personal hygiene routines during their care. For meals, I prepared ingredients and laid them out with sticky notes containing simple cooking instructions after breakfast. This helped Kay maintain her independence and ensured they both had balanced meals.

Evening walks had been part of their daily routine since Kay's diabetes diagnosis. As their physical abilities declined, we introduced indoor exercises with written instructions to keep them active. As Mike and Kay's mental faculties began to wane, establishing a routine became crucial. Convincing them to bathe was challenging and met with resistance, but sticking to a structured routine effectively managed their care.

PHYSICAL HEALTH MATTERS

In this chapter, we embark on a journey dedicated to nurturing and safeguarding the physical well-being of aging parents. As caregivers, ensuring the vitality and comfort of our loved ones becomes a top priority. From managing chronic conditions to promoting healthy lifestyle choices, this chapter provides a comprehensive guide to addressing the multifaceted aspects of physical health in elderly care.

Throughout these pages, we explore practical strategies, expert advice, and insights to empower you in providing the best possible care for your parents. Whether it's navigating medication regimens, addressing mobility challenges, or fostering an environment conducive to wellness, we're here to support you every step of the way.

Join us as we delve into the heart of caregiving, where compassion meets action. Together, let's embark on a journey toward enhancing your aging parents' physical health and vitality.

COMMON ILLNESSES

As our parents age, they become more susceptible to various health conditions and illnesses. As a caregiver, it's crucial to know the common illnesses your aging parents may encounter, like heart disease, diabetes, arthritis, dementia, and respiratory issues. Knowing their symptoms, treatment options, and preventive measures can help you provide better support and ensure their well-being.

By staying proactive, educated, and communicating regularly with healthcare professionals, you can promote your parents' health and improve their quality of life.

Some common health issues that aging parents may experience include:

- **Arthritis:** Arthritis causes inflammation and stiffness in the joints, leading to pain and reduced mobility. It can affect different joints in the body and worsen over time.
- **High blood pressure (hypertension):** High blood pressure, or hypertension, is when the force of blood against artery walls is consistently too high. It often shows no symptoms but can lead to serious health issues like heart disease and stroke if untreated. Lifestyle changes and medication can help manage it.
- **Diabetes:** Type 2 diabetes is more common in older adults and can lead to serious complications if not properly managed. It requires careful monitoring of

blood sugar levels and adherence to a healthy lifestyle and medication regimen.

- **Osteoporosis:** Osteoporosis is a condition characterized by weak and brittle bones, which increases the risk of fractures, especially in older adults and women after menopause.
- **Heart disease:** Aging increases the risk of heart disease, including conditions such as coronary artery disease, heart failure, and arrhythmias. Managing risk factors such as high blood pressure, high cholesterol, and diabetes is crucial for preventing heart disease.
- **Dementia:** Dementia, including Alzheimer's disease, is a progressive condition that affects memory, cognition, and behavior. It can significantly impact daily functioning and quality of life for the individual and their caregivers.
- **Depression:** Depression is common among older adults, often as a result of life changes, chronic illness, or social isolation. Recognizing the signs of depression and seeking appropriate treatment and support is essential for mental well-being.
- **Vision and hearing loss:** Aging often leads to changes in vision and hearing, such as cataracts, macular degeneration, and presbycusis (age-related hearing loss). Regular eye and ear exams can help detect and manage these conditions.
- **Respiratory issues:** Chronic respiratory conditions such as chronic obstructive pulmonary disease (COPD) and pneumonia are more common in older adults and can significantly impact breathing and overall health.

- **Cancer:** The risk of cancer increases with age, and older adults may develop various types of cancer, including lung, breast, prostate, colorectal, and skin cancer. Early detection and treatment are critical for improving outcomes.

MANAGING COMMON ILLNESSES

Managing common illnesses in aging parents requires a combination of proactive preventive measures, ongoing management, and supportive care. A proactive and holistic approach to managing your aging parents' health can help them maintain their well-being, independence, and quality of life as they age. It's important to involve your parents in their care decisions and respect their preferences and autonomy.

Here are some strategies to help you effectively manage your parents' health conditions:

- **Regular medical checkups:** Schedule regular checkups with healthcare providers to monitor your parents' health status, manage chronic conditions, and address new concerns or symptoms.
- **Medication management:** Ensure your parents take their medications as prescribed and regularly refill prescriptions. Organize pillboxes, set reminders, and communicate with healthcare providers about any concerns or side effects.
- **Healthy lifestyle:** Encourage your parents to maintain a healthy lifestyle by eating a balanced diet, staying physically active, managing stress, avoiding

tobacco and excessive alcohol consumption, and getting adequate sleep.

- **Fall prevention:** Minimize fall risks by removing tripping hazards in their living environment, installing grab bars in bathrooms, using nonslip mats, and encouraging mobility aids if necessary.
- **Supportive devices:** Provide assistive devices and equipment as needed, such as walkers, canes, hearing aids, and eyeglasses, to help your parents maintain independence and function safely.
- **Home modifications:** Consider modifying your parents' home to accommodate their changing needs, such as installing ramps, stairlifts, and bathroom grab bars or arranging home healthcare services if necessary.
- **Emotional support:** Offer emotional support and reassurance to your parents as they navigate the challenges of managing their health conditions. Listen to their concerns and encourage them to make decisions about their care.
- **Social engagement:** Encourage social interaction and engagement with friends, family, and community activities to prevent social isolation and promote mental well-being.
- **Education:** Learn about your parents' health conditions, treatment options, and available support resources to help you make informed decisions and effectively advocate for their needs.
- **Care coordination:** Coordinate care between healthcare providers, specialists, and other support services involved in your parents' care to ensure

continuity and comprehensive management of their health conditions.

Bathing and Grooming

When bathing and grooming an elderly loved one, it's essential to approach the process with sensitivity and respect. One tip is to create a warm and comfortable environment, using soft towels and gentle lighting to promote relaxation.

Additionally, communicating effectively and involving your loved one in decision-making can help maintain their dignity. It's also crucial to ensure their safety by using nonslip mats and grab bars in the bathroom. Gentle and thorough care while being mindful of physical limitations can provide a positive and dignified experience for your aging loved one:

- **Put safety first:** Make safety a top priority by ensuring the bathroom is equipped with essential features such as grab bars and nonslip mats. This helps prevent accidents and provides a secure environment.
- **Respect privacy:** Respect your loved one's privacy throughout the process. Use privacy screens or close the door to create a private space, allowing them to maintain their dignity and comfort.
- **Prepare all supplies:** Gather all necessary supplies beforehand to streamline the process. This includes towels, soap, shampoo, and grooming tools. Having everything prepared reduces stress and makes the experience more efficient.

- **Have an open conversation:** Maintain open communication with your loved one about their preferences and comfort level. Discussing the bathing and grooming routine beforehand helps address concerns and ensures a collaborative approach.
- **Be patient and respectful:** Approach the task with patience and respect, understanding that your loved one may take time to adjust. Allow them to participate as much as possible and be attentive to their needs and preferences.

Following these tips can help ensure that bathing and grooming become positive and comfortable experiences for you and your aging loved one.

EMPOWERING AGING PARENTS: RESPECTFUL STRATEGIES FOR BATHING AND GROOMING

Taking care of your aging parents' bathing and grooming habits requires sensitivity, respect for their dignity, and consideration for physical limitations. Here are some tips to help you assist your aging parents with bathing and grooming in a supportive and respectful manner:

- **Communicate:** Have open and honest conversations with your parents about their preferences and concerns regarding bathing and grooming assistance. Respect their autonomy and involve them in decisions about their care whenever possible.

- **Establish a routine:** Create a regular bathing and grooming schedule that works for you and your parents. Consistency can help alleviate anxiety and make the process more predictable for everyone involved.
- **Ensure safety:** Make the bathing area safe and accessible by installing grab bars, nonslip mats, and shower chairs if needed. Adjust water temperature to a comfortable level and provide adequate lighting.
- **Respect privacy:** Maintain your parent's privacy by closing doors and curtains during bathing and grooming activities. Use towels or robes to cover areas of the body not being washed and provide modesty garments if desired.
- **Assist as needed:** Offer assistance with tasks such as getting in and out of the shower or bath, washing hard-to-reach areas, shampooing hair, and drying off. Be patient and gentle, and allow your parent to do as much as they can independently.
- **Use gentle products:** Choose mild and hypoallergenic soap, shampoo, and skincare products suitable for aging skin. Avoid products that may cause irritation or dryness.
- **Respect personal preferences:** Be mindful of your parent's grooming preferences, such as hairstyle, clothing choices, and grooming routines. Respect their individuality and assist them in maintaining their preferred appearance.
- **Be attentive:** Pay attention to any discomfort or pain during bathing and grooming activities. Be responsive to your parent's needs and adjust your approach accordingly.

- **Seek professional help if needed:** If bathing and grooming tasks become too challenging or your parent requires specialized care, consider enlisting the help of a professional caregiver or home healthcare aide.
- **Offer emotional support:** Show empathy and understanding toward your parent's feelings about aging and needing assistance with personal care tasks. Offer reassurance and encouragement to help them feel comfortable and confident.

By approaching bathing and grooming with compassion, respect, and sensitivity, you can help your aging parents maintain their hygiene and dignity while ensuring their safety and well-being.

BATHING SAFELY

Bathing elderly parents can be sensitive and challenging, but the right approach can be a positive and respectful experience for both parties. Here are 10 tips for helping bathe elderly parents safely and respectfully:

- **Maintain open communication:** Discuss bathing preferences with your parent beforehand, allowing them to express their comfort levels and preferences.
- **Install shower aides:** Consider installing safety aids like shower rails or walk-in tubs to enhance safety and accessibility during bathing.
- **Respect privacy:** Allow for privacy when possible, enabling your parent to maintain independence in personal hygiene.

- **Utilize safety tools:** Use portable devices like shower chairs to assist seniors with difficulty navigating the bathroom.
- **Prepare beforehand:** Prepare bathing supplies and set up the bathroom in advance to streamline the bathing process and reduce stress.
- **Establish a routine:** Create a consistent bathing schedule to provide structure and reduce anxiety for your elderly parent.
- **Ensure thorough cleansing:** Pay attention to cleaning inside skin folds to ensure thorough cleanliness during bathing.
- **Rinse adequately:** Rinse off soap thoroughly to prevent skin irritation and discomfort.
- **Choose comfortable attire:** Have clean and comfortable clothes ready for your parents to wear after bathing, promoting comfort and well-being.
- **Adapt to needs:** Adjust bathing frequency and methods based on your parents' preferences and needs, prioritizing their comfort and overall health.

MEALS

When meal planning for your aging parents, focusing on nutritious and easy-to-digest foods that support their health and well-being is essential. By focusing on nutritious foods, planning balanced meals, and exploring new recipes, you can ensure your aging parents receive the nourishment they need to thrive. Making mealtime enjoyable and satisfying contributes to their overall health and well-being.

Here are some personalized meal-planning ideas to consider:

- **Choose the best types of foods:** Prioritize nutrient-dense foods rich in vitamins, minerals, and antioxidants. Their diet should include plenty of fruits, vegetables, whole grains, lean proteins, and healthy fats to support overall health and vitality.
- **Make a 7-day meal plan:** Create a weekly meal plan that incorporates a variety of nutritious meals and snacks. Each meal should balance protein, carbohydrates, and healthy fats to sustain energy and promote satiety—plan for simple, easy-to-prepare meals that are flavorful and satisfying.
- **Find easy recipes to prepare:** Expand your recipe repertoire with simple and nourishing dishes that your parents will love. Consider hearty soups, nutrient-packed salads, flavorful stir-fries, and comforting casseroles. Opt for recipes that use fresh, seasonal ingredients and can be prepared in advance for convenience.

General Meal Plan

When planning meals for your parents, be flexible and accommodating to their preferences while promoting healthy eating habits. Encourage them to enjoy meals together as a family whenever possible, as social interaction can enhance the dining experience and overall well-being.

Here's a general meal plan template to consider:

Breakfast

- whole-grain cereal or oatmeal topped with fresh fruit and nuts
- low-fat yogurt or cottage cheese
- whole-grain toast or whole wheat English muffin with peanut butter or avocado
- herbal tea or low-fat milk

Mid-Morning Snack

- fresh fruit such as apple slices, berries, or banana
- handful of almonds or walnuts
- low-fat yogurt or cheese stick

Lunch

- grilled chicken or fish with steamed vegetables
- quinoa or brown rice
- mixed green salad with a variety of vegetables and vinaigrette dressing
- whole-grain roll or whole-wheat pita bread
- water or herbal tea

Afternoon Snack

- whole-grain crackers with hummus or guacamole
- baby carrots or celery sticks with almond butter
- Greek yogurt with honey and granola

Dinner

- baked salmon or tofu with roasted sweet potatoes and broccoli
- mixed bean salad with bell peppers, tomatoes, and olive oil dressing
- whole-grain pasta with marinara sauce and a side of steamed spinach
- whole-grain dinner roll or whole-wheat tortilla
- water or herbal tea

Evening Snack (Optional)

- sliced fruit with a dollop of Greek yogurt
- air-popped popcorn
- herbal tea or decaffeinated beverage

Important Considerations

- Ensure meals are well-balanced with lean protein, whole grains, fruits, vegetables, and healthy fats.
- Encourage hydration by offering water throughout the day and limiting sugary beverages.
- Consider any dietary restrictions or preferences your parents may have, such as low-sodium, low-fat, or vegetarian options.
- Remember that portion control is essential, especially for older adults with reduced calorie needs.
- Consult with a healthcare provider or registered dietitian for personalized dietary recommendations

based on your parents' health conditions, medications, and nutritional needs.

WHAT IF THEY HAVE LIMITED MOBILITY?

When caring for aging parents with limited mobility, it's essential to understand the root cause of their mobility issues and explore strategies to improve or manage their condition. Here's a personal approach to addressing these concerns:

- **Do you understand the root of the mobility problem?** Take time to understand the underlying factors contributing to your parent's limited mobility. This may include chronic conditions, injuries, or age-related changes in strength and flexibility. Consulting with healthcare professionals can provide valuable insights and guidance.
- **Can older people regain mobility?** While some mobility issues may be irreversible, many seniors can improve their mobility with the right interventions. Physical therapy, regular exercise, assistive devices, and lifestyle modifications can help seniors regain strength, flexibility, and independence.
- **What helps older adults with weak legs?** Strengthening exercises, such as leg lifts, squats, and resistance training, can help improve leg strength and stability. Additionally, assistive devices like walkers, canes, or scooters can support and enhance mobility.

- **How do you care for the immobile elderly?** Caring for immobile seniors requires patience, compassion, and specialized assistance. To maintain overall well-being, ensure their living environment is safe and accessible, assist with daily activities, and promote social engagement and mental stimulation.
- **What mobility aids are available for elderly parents?** Various aids are available to help elderly parents navigate their surroundings safely. These include walkers, rollators, canes, wheelchairs, and stairlifts. Choosing the right aid depends on your parent's specific needs and level of mobility.

By addressing the root cause of mobility issues, exploring options for improvement, and providing appropriate support and assistance, you can help your aging parents maintain mobility and independence for as long as possible. You can make a positive difference in their quality of life with patience, empathy, and proactive care.

Keep Them Moving

Movement and physical activity are essential for aging parents' mobility and well-being. Here are some personalized exercises and stretches to keep them moving:

- **Upper body clam shell:** Sit comfortably with your arms at your sides. Slowly lift both arms to the sides, then return to the starting position. Repeat for a set number of repetitions.

- **Semi-sits:** Sit on the edge of a chair with feet flat on the floor. Lean forward slightly, then push through your heels to stand halfway up before sitting back down. This strengthens leg muscles.
- **Seated abdominal press:** Sit tall with hands on your thighs. Press your hands into your thighs while engaging your core muscles. Hold for a few seconds, then release. Repeat several times.
- **Side bends:** Sit upright with feet flat on the floor. Gently lean to one side, reaching towards the floor while keeping the opposite hand overhead. Return to the starting position and repeat on the other side.
- **Low-back rotation stretch:** Sit tall in a chair with feet flat on the floor. Slowly twist your torso to one side, using your hands on the armrests for support. Hold the stretch for a few seconds, then return to the center and repeat on the other side.
- **Wrist and ankle rolls:** Rotate wrists and ankles in circular motions to improve joint mobility and flexibility.
- **Knee marches:** Sit tall with feet flat on the floor. Lift one knee toward your chest, then lower it back down and repeat with the other knee. Alternate between legs for a set number of repetitions.
- **Seated rows:** Sit tall with a resistance band wrapped around your feet. Hold the ends of the band with both hands, palms facing each other. Pull the band toward your chest, squeezing your shoulder blades together. Slowly release and repeat.

- **Arm raises:** Sit tall with arms at your sides. Slowly raise both arms to the sides and overhead, then lower them back down. Repeat for a set number of repetitions to improve shoulder mobility.
- **Seated torso twist:** Sit tall with feet flat on the floor. Place one hand on the opposite knee and gently twist your torso toward that side. Hold the stretch for a few seconds, then return to the center and repeat on the other side.
- **Inner thigh and hand squeeze:** Sit tall with a small ball or cushion between your knees. Squeeze the ball with your inner thighs while simultaneously squeezing a hand gripper or stress ball with your hands.
- **Calf raises:** Sit tall with feet flat on the floor. Lift your heels off the ground, rising onto the balls of your feet. Hold for a few seconds, then lower back down. Repeat for a set number of repetitions to strengthen calf muscles.

It's important to encourage your aging parents to add exercises and stretches to their daily routine to enhance their mobility, flexibility, and overall physical function. However, it's always advisable to consult a healthcare professional before starting any new exercise program, particularly for individuals with mobility issues or underlying health conditions.

This chapter explored caring for your parents' physical health. Please remember that while this might not always be an easy task, and there will likely be days when you want to pull your hair out, you can do this! Also, remember that this selfless act is one that you will always be grateful for taking on.

The next chapter explores caring for your parents' psychological needs. Grab a warm cuppa and get comfy as you learn more about your parents' needs.

UNLOCK THE POWER OF GENEROSITY

Kindness is the language which the deaf can hear and the blind can see.

— MARK TWAIN

People who give without expectation live longer, happier lives and add value to their community.

With that in mind, I have a question for you...

Would you help someone you've never met, even if you never got credit for it?

Who is this person, you ask? They are like you—or, at least, like you used to be—less experienced, wanting to make a difference, and needing help but unsure where to look.

My mission is to make my caregiving strategies accessible to everyone. This book stems from that mission, and the only way for me to accomplish it is by reaching... everyone.

This is where you come in. Most people do, in fact, judge a book by its cover (and its reviews). So, here's my ask on behalf of every struggling caregiver you've never met:

Please help that caregiver by leaving this book a review.

Your gift costs no money and less than 60 seconds to make, but it can change a fellow caregiver's life forever. Your review could help...

...one more family finds the support they need...one more caregiver feels confident in their role...one more elderly parent receives the care they deserve...one more dream of a better life comes true.

To get that 'feel good' feeling and help this person for real, simply leave a review, which takes less than 60 seconds.

Simply scan the QR code to leave your review:

Leave a review!

If you feel good about helping a faceless caregiver, you are my kind of person. Welcome to the club. You're one of us.

I'm even more excited to help you care for your aging parents with more confidence than you can possibly imagine. You'll love the tips and strategies I share in the coming chapters.

Thank you from the bottom of my heart.

Kim Livingston

PS—Fun fact: If you provide something of value to another person, it makes you more valuable to them. If you'd like to share goodwill directly with another caregiver—and you believe this book will help them—send it their way.

5

STRENGTHEN THEIR MINDS

It wasn't long into our caregiving journey that we noticed Mike showing signs of agitation at his inability to remember simple things. He began repeating the same questions. When we would answer, he acted as if it was the first time he had asked. We also noticed that he was beginning to shuffle his feet before he would take a step. It was almost like he couldn't get started, like his feet were sticking to the ground.

This sudden change prompted us to make an appointment with his primary care physician, who referred us to a neurologist. After several tests, the neurologist reported no significant findings. Discouraged, we had no real answers to what seemed to be a sudden mental and physical change. Someone then recommended we make an appointment with a psychiatrist.

At first, we didn't feel it appropriate to seek psychiatric counseling for what appeared to be a neurological issue. But we had nothing to lose, so we reluctantly made the appointment. To our surprise, we gained more insight, had more answers to what was happening with Mike, and received a perspective on what to look forward to over time. The psychiatrist took the time to speak with the four of us as a family.

This was the most informative appointment and helped us become more prepared for the road ahead on our journey. Not only did this help us understand what was immediately happening with Mike, but it also helped us understand what was likely to be expected. We also gained insight into some emotions and anxiety we, as caregivers, were experiencing. I highly recommend anyone taking this journey to seek out a psychiatrist who specializes in dementia and short-term memory loss early in your journey.

PSYCHOLOGICAL NEEDS

As parents age, it's important to prioritize their mental well-being. Just like exercising to keep your body strong, there are various ways to help strengthen your parents' minds. From stimulating activities to social engagement, nurturing cognitive health can enhance their quality of life and independence. Investing in your parents' cognitive health through brain exercises, social interactions, or lifelong learning can lead to a more fulfilling aging journey.

Prioritizing your parents' mental and emotional health needs enhances their well-being and strengthens family dynamics and caregiving relationships. Taking care of your parents' mental and emotional health needs is crucial for several reasons:

- **Quality of life:** Addressing their mental and emotional well-being enhances their overall quality of life, promoting happiness and fulfillment in their later years.
- **Physical health:** Mental and emotional health directly impact physical health. Addressing stress, anxiety, and depression can contribute to better physical health outcomes and overall well-being.
- **Relationship dynamics:** Maintaining good mental and emotional health fosters positive relationships with family members, caregivers, and peers, improving communication and reducing conflicts.
- **Cognitive function:** Mental and emotional health influences cognitive function and resilience. You can help maintain cognitive abilities and delay cognitive decline by addressing their needs in these areas.
- **Adaptability to change:** Aging comes with significant life changes, like health challenges or loss of independence. Robust mental and emotional health can help your parents navigate these changes more effectively and adapt to new circumstances.

MENTAL AND EMOTIONAL HEALTH NEEDS

- **Create a mental health care plan:** Work with healthcare professionals to craft a personalized mental health plan for your parents, adapting it to maintain its efficacy.
- **Eat well and get enough sleep:** To support mental and emotional health, encourage healthy eating,

regular meals, hydration, a consistent sleep schedule, and comfortable sleep.

- **Get physical:** Encourage enjoyable physical activities like walking, swimming, gardening, or yoga for stress relief and mood improvement. Offer companionship for motivation.
- **Adopt a pet:** Consider adopting or arranging visits with pets for parents. Assess capabilities and preferences beforehand, including allergies and mobility.
- **Keep an active mind:** Encourage hobbies for mental stimulation. Support new interests and socialization. Challenge them with puzzles, games, learning, memory exercises, and conversations.
- **Stay connected:** Encourage social connections with family, friends, and community. Plan visits, calls, or activities for a sense of belonging.

DEMENTIA

Dementia is characterized by a decline in cognitive function that affects memory, thinking, behavior, and the ability to perform everyday activities. It's common among seniors and often associated with aging but is not considered normal.

When communicating with someone with dementia, it's important to approach interactions with patience, empathy, and understanding. Here are some tips:

- **Maintain a calm demeanor:** Speak gently and reassuringly, and remain patient even if they become confused or repeat themselves.

- **Use simple language:** Keep your sentences short and straightforward. Avoid using complex or abstract language that might be difficult for them to understand.
- **Give them time to respond:** Allow them extra time to process information and formulate responses. Avoid rushing or interrupting them.
- **Use nonverbal cues:** Pay attention to your body language and facial expressions. Maintain eye contact and use gestures to help convey your message.
- **Focus on feelings:** Instead of correcting misinformation or challenging their reality, focus on validating their feelings and providing emotional support.
- **Be a good listener:** Encourage them to express themselves and listen attentively to what they have to say. Show empathy and understanding, even if you don't fully comprehend their perspective.
- **Avoid distractions:** Minimize distractions like background noise or competing conversations, as these can make it harder for them to concentrate and communicate effectively.
- **Be patient and flexible:** Understand that their abilities may fluctuate daily, and be prepared to adapt your communication approach accordingly.
- **Use memory aids:** Utilize memory aids like photographs, familiar objects, or written notes to help stimulate their memory and facilitate communication.

- **Seek support:** Seek guidance from healthcare professionals or join a caregiver support group for valuable advice and resources in communicating with a parent with dementia.

PARKINSON'S

Parkinson's disease affects movement and is caused by damage to nerve cells that produce dopamine in the brain. This results in a range of motor symptoms, such as tremors, stiffness, slow movement, difficulty with balance and coordination, and non-motor symptoms, like cognitive changes, mood disorders, and sleep disturbances.

Seniors with Parkinson's should work closely with a healthcare team to develop a comprehensive treatment plan tailored to their needs and goals. Early intervention and ongoing management can help optimize symptom control and maintain quality of life for people living with Parkinson's disease.

Treatment for Parkinson's disease aims to manage symptoms and improve quality of life. Here are some common approaches:

- **Medications:** The primary treatment for Parkinson's involves medications that help replenish dopamine levels in the brain or mimic its effects. These may include levodopa, dopamine agonists, MAO-B, and COMT inhibitors. These medications can help alleviate motor symptoms and improve movement control.

- **Deep brain stimulation (DBS):** DBS is a surgical procedure that involves implanting electrodes in specific brain areas responsible for movement control. These electrodes deliver electrical impulses to help regulate abnormal brain activity associated with Parkinson's symptoms. DBS can be effective in reducing motor fluctuations and tremors in individuals who do not respond well to medication alone.
- **Physical therapy:** Physical therapy can help improve mobility, flexibility, and balance in people with Parkinson's disease. Therapists can teach exercises and techniques to manage symptoms and maintain independence in daily activities.
- **Occupational therapy:** Occupational therapists can provide strategies and adaptations to help seniors with Parkinson's disease maintain their ability to perform activities of daily living, like dressing, bathing, and eating. They can also recommend assistive devices and modifications to the home environment to improve safety and accessibility.
- **Speech therapy:** Speech therapists can assist individuals with Parkinson's disease who experience speech and swallowing difficulties. They can provide exercises to strengthen muscles involved in speech and swallowing and techniques to improve communication and prevent aspiration.
- **Exercise:** Regular exercise, like walking, swimming, or cycling, can help improve muscle strength, flexibility, and balance in people with Parkinson's. Exercise has also been shown to have

neuroprotective effects and may slow disease progression.

- **Nutrition and lifestyle modifications:** Eating a balanced diet and staying hydrated can help manage symptoms and support overall health. Some people with Parkinson's disease find that certain dietary supplements or alternative therapies, like acupuncture or yoga, provide additional relief from symptoms.

- **Supportive care:** Supportive care services, like counseling, support groups, and palliative care, can help seniors and their families cope with the emotional and practical challenges of living with Parkinson's disease.

Helping Your Parents Cope

Helping your parents cope with aging and associated challenges requires patience, empathy, and proactive support. By staying involved, seeking support, respecting independence, planning care together, and maintaining perspective, you can help your parents cope with the challenges of aging while preserving their dignity and autonomy.

Here are ways you can assist your parents in coping:

- **Stay involved:** Maintain regular communication and spend quality time with your parents. Offer emotional support, companionship, and reassurance as they navigate aging.

- **Find support:** Join support groups, counseling, or online communities for yourself and your parents to gain valuable advice and empathy.
- **Respect independence:** Respect your parents' autonomy. Avoid taking over tasks or making decisions without their input.
- **Plan care together:** Involve parents in care planning and create a plan that meets their needs and respects their wishes.
- **Maintain perspective:** Cherish your parents despite physical or cognitive changes, and create meaningful moments together.

DEPRESSION

Depression in seniors, often referred to as late-life depression or geriatric depression, is a mental health disorder characterized by persistent feelings of sadness, hopelessness, and loss of interest or pleasure in once enjoyable activities. It can occur in older adults due to a variety of factors, including biological, psychological, and social aspects, as well as life changes like retirement, loss of loved ones, or chronic illness.

Symptoms of depression in seniors may differ from those in younger adults and can include:

- persistent sadness or low mood
- loss of interest or pleasure in activities
- changes in appetite or weight
- sleep disturbances (insomnia or excessive sleeping)
- fatigue or loss of energy

- feelings of worthlessness or guilt
- difficulty concentrating or making decisions
- thoughts of death or suicide

Depression in seniors is often underdiagnosed and under-treated, as it can be mistaken for normal aging or other medical conditions. A combination of approaches tailored to the individual's needs and circumstances is often most effective in treating depression in seniors. Seniors and their families need to recognize the signs of depression and seek help from healthcare professionals for assessment and treatment. With proper support and treatment, many older adults can experience significant improvement in their symptoms and quality of life.

Depression, however, is a treatable condition, and there are several effective approaches:

- **Psychotherapy:** Talk therapy, like cognitive-behavioral therapy (CBT) or interpersonal therapy (IPT), can be highly effective in treating depression in seniors. Therapy sessions can help seniors identify and challenge negative thought patterns, develop coping skills, and address underlying issues contributing to their depression.
- **Medications:** Antidepressant medications, like selective serotonin reuptake inhibitors (SSRIs) or serotonin-norepinephrine reuptake inhibitors (SNRIs), may be prescribed to help alleviate symptoms of depression. Seniors must work closely with their healthcare provider to find the right

medication and dosage, as older adults may be more sensitive to side effects.

- **Social support:** Maintaining social connections and participating in social activities can help combat feelings of loneliness and isolation, which are common contributors to depression in seniors. Family, friends, and support groups can provide emotional support and companionship.
- **Physical activity:** Regular exercise is beneficial for both physical and mental health, including reducing symptoms of depression. Seniors should engage in activities they enjoy, like walking, swimming, or yoga, to improve mood and overall well-being.
- **Healthy lifestyle habits:** Eating a balanced diet, getting adequate sleep, and avoiding alcohol and substance abuse can help support mental health and reduce symptoms of depression.
- **Treatment of underlying medical conditions:** Chronic health conditions like diabetes, heart disease, or thyroid disorders can contribute to depression in seniors. Managing these conditions effectively through medication, lifestyle changes, and regular medical care can help alleviate depressive symptoms.
- **Supportive services:** Seniors may benefit from additional support services, such as home healthcare, meal delivery, or transportation assistance, to help them maintain independence and cope with the challenges of aging.
- **Regular monitoring and follow-up:** Seniors with depression need to receive ongoing monitoring and follow-up care from healthcare providers to ensure

that treatment is effective and to address any changes in symptoms or medication needs.

ANXIETY

Anxiety in seniors is a mental health condition characterized by persistent worry, fear, or apprehension that is disproportionate to the situation and interferes with daily functioning. It can manifest in various forms, including generalized anxiety disorder (GAD), panic disorder, phobias, or social anxiety disorder. Anxiety in seniors may be triggered by factors like health concerns, changes in living situations, loss of independence, or worries about the future.

Symptoms of anxiety in seniors may include:

- excessive worrying about everyday matters
- restlessness or feeling on edge
- difficulty concentrating or making decisions
- irritability or agitation
- muscle tension or aches
- fatigue or trouble sleeping
- rapid heartbeat or shortness of breath
- gastrointestinal problems, like stomachaches or nausea

Helping your parents cope with anxiety involves a combination of supportive interventions and professional assistance. By implementing these strategies and offering support and encouragement, you can help seniors cope with anxiety and improve their overall quality of life. Here are some strategies to help seniors manage anxiety:

- **Encourage open communication:** Create a safe and supportive environment where seniors feel comfortable expressing their feelings and concerns. Encourage them to talk about what's bothering them and listen attentively without judgment.

- **Provide reassurance:** Offer encouragement and reassurance to help alleviate worries and fears. Let them know that their feelings are valid and that they are not alone.

- **Promote relaxation techniques:** Teach your parents relaxation techniques like deep breathing exercises, progressive muscle relaxation, or mindfulness meditation. These techniques can help reduce stress and promote a sense of calmness and well-being.

- **Encourage physical activity:** Regular exercise can help reduce anxiety symptoms by releasing endorphins, improving mood, and promoting relaxation. Encourage seniors to engage in physical activities they enjoy, such as walking, gardening, or gentle yoga.

- **Establish a routine:** Structure and predictability can help reduce anxiety in seniors. Establishing a daily routine for activities such as meals, exercise, and socializing can provide a sense of stability and control.

- **Promote social connections:** Encourage seniors to maintain connections with family, friends, and community groups. Social support can reduce loneliness and isolation and provide meaningful interaction and companionship opportunities.

- **Address underlying health issues:** Anxiety in seniors may be exacerbated by underlying health conditions like chronic pain, sleep disturbances, or medication side effects. Work with healthcare providers to address these issues and optimize treatment to alleviate anxiety symptoms.
- **Seek professional help:** If anxiety symptoms persist or significantly impact daily functioning, encourage seniors to seek professional help from a mental health professional, like a therapist or psychiatrist. Cognitive-behavioral therapy (CBT), medication, or other evidence-based treatments may be recommended based on the individual's needs and preferences.
- **Educate caregivers:** Provide education and support to caregivers, family members, and other support networks to help them understand anxiety in seniors and how to best support their loved ones.
- **Promote self-care:** Encourage seniors to prioritize self-care activities such as adequate sleep, healthy eating, and engaging in hobbies and interests that bring them joy and fulfillment.

DELIRIUM

Delirium is a sudden and severe change in mental function that often occurs in older adults, particularly those who are hospitalized or have underlying medical conditions. It is characterized by disturbances in attention, awareness, and cognition and may also involve hallucinations, delusions, or changes in perception. Delirium can fluctuate in severity throughout the day and is typically caused by an underlying medical condition, medication side effects, or environmental factors.

Symptoms of delirium in seniors may include:

- confusion or disorientation
- inability to focus or maintain attention
- altered perception of reality (hallucinations or delusions)
- agitation or restlessness
- fluctuations in alertness or consciousness
- impaired memory or language skills
- sleep disturbances
- changes in behavior or personality

If you suspect a senior is experiencing delirium, seeking medical attention promptly is essential. Delirium can be a medical emergency and may indicate a serious underlying condition.

By providing a supportive and safe environment, minimizing stressors, and addressing the underlying causes of delirium, you can help seniors cope with this challenging condition and improve their overall well-being. Here are some ways to help seniors cope with delirium:

- **Ensure safety:** Ensure the environment is safe and free from hazards that could potentially harm the senior, like sharp objects, slippery floors, or obstacles in the walkway. Assist with mobility if needed to prevent falls or injuries.

- **Reorient as needed:** Help the senior maintain a sense of orientation by providing frequent reminders of the time, place, and situation. Use calendars, clocks, and familiar objects to help ground them in reality and reduce confusion.
- **Minimize stimulation:** Reduce excessive noise, light, and activity in the environment to help minimize distractions and agitation. Create a calm and quiet atmosphere to promote relaxation and improve focus.
- **Ensure adequate hydration and nutrition:** Encourage the senior to drink fluids and eat nutritious meals to maintain hydration and energy levels. If the senior's appetite is poor, offer small, frequent meals and snacks.
- **Promote rest and sleep:** Ensure the senior gets adequate rest and sleep by providing a comfortable sleeping environment and a regular sleep schedule. Minimize disruptions during nighttime hours to promote uninterrupted sleep.
- **Stay calm and reassuring:** Approach interactions with the senior calmly, gently, and reassuringly. Speak in a soothing tone of voice and provide emotional support to help alleviate anxiety and agitation.
- **Engage in familiar activities:** Encourage the senior to engage in familiar activities or hobbies, like listening to music, looking at photo albums, or doing puzzles. These activities provide a sense of comfort and familiarity.

- **Monitor for changes:** Monitor the senior's symptoms and behavior closely and promptly report any changes or worsening of delirium symptoms to healthcare providers. Delirium can be a sign of an underlying medical problem that requires prompt evaluation and treatment.
- **Involve healthcare providers:** Work closely with healthcare providers, including doctors, nurses, and other members of the healthcare team, to address the underlying causes of delirium and develop a comprehensive treatment plan. This may involve adjusting medications, treating infections, or managing other medical conditions contributing to delirium.

The chapter emphasizes the importance of supporting aging parents' mental and cognitive well-being. It advises encouraging hobbies for stimulation and fulfillment while promoting socialization. Additionally, it suggests engaging in activities and seeking guidance from healthcare professionals or caregiver support groups when communication becomes challenging, especially in dementia cases.

Chapter 6 dives into the essential strategies for managing healthcare effectively, empowering you to navigate medical appointments, treatments, and decisions confidently and professionally. Learn valuable tips and tools to advocate for your parents' health and make informed decisions like a pro.

MANAGE HEALTHCARE LIKE A PRO

I t is crucial to attend the healthcare visits with your parents. Advocating for their care requires detailed communication with the physician regarding your observations and experiences at home. Your parents may not share critical information because they are unwilling, may not think it's important, or forget. Additionally, they may not follow the doctor's instructions because they cannot understand or forget.

As discussed in Chapter 4, Kay's background as an RN led us to believe she was fully communicative about her health issues, especially concerning her diabetes. However, it wasn't until Sam and I started attending her endocrinology appointments that we realized she hadn't been disclosing some crucial information about her struggles with glucose management.

Unaware of these issues, her doctor could not provide appropriate management advice, which only compounded the problems. Our presence at the appointments allowed us to convey these issues effectively, enabling her doctor to offer specific guidance on managing her diabetes more effectively.

I also offer a practical tip: Secure authorization to discuss your parents' medical insurance and Medicare. Insurance complexities can be daunting, and your parents may need assistance with billing inquiries. By contacting Medicare and any secondary insurers and explaining that you are the caregiver, they will provide a form for your parents to sign and notarize.

This authorization allows you to handle insurance coverage and billing issues on their behalf. It is crucial to arrange this while your parents are still able to give consent. We found that Medicare and the secondary insurers were very supportive, and securing this authorization early helped us efficiently manage the insurance aspects of their care.

MANAGING MEDICATION

It's alarming that almost half of all adults aged 65 and above manage five or more medications simultaneously. This can be a struggle, especially for seniors with cognitive issues. As a caregiver, you can help manage your parent's medication and prevent mishaps like missed doses or overdoses. These simple steps can organize prescriptions and keep schedules on track, emphasizing your crucial role in their health journey.

Consult With Your Parent's Doctor

Around 15% of ER visits among older adults are due to adverse drug reactions. Since seniors consult multiple doctors, ensuring no medication conflicts is essential. Accompanying your parent to medical appointments allows for thorough medication review and dosage adjustments if needed. Ask each doctor about simplifying medication and inform them about any over-the-counter medicines your parent uses.

Track Medications

Once you've discussed this with your parent's medical team, take a moment to compile a detailed list of all prescribed medications. Create a phone list to track medications for your parent. Keep a copy on hand and share it with everyone involved in their care to stay informed and organized. This list should include details like:

- the name of each medication of each parent
- the prescribed dosage
- instructions on how and when to take each medication
- any special instructions, like taking it before bedtime
- potential side effects or contraindications

Medication Tracking Apps

Use a medication tracking app like Med-Helper or Medisafe to stick to your parent's medication schedule. These apps offer helpful features like medication logs, alerts for missed doses, warnings about drug interactions, and reminders for prescription refills. They also make it easy to coordinate care with other caregivers.

Keep Medications Properly Organized

Store medications on a kitchen counter instead of a bathroom cabinet. Refrigerate medicines on an easy-to-reach shelf. Invest in an organizer for easy accessibility, and use separate ones for different times of the day.

Establish Routine

Align your parent's medication schedule with their daily routine. Determine the best time for administering their medication by considering their habits. Manage their medication with organization and preparation, using practical tips to ensure their safety and well-being.

WHAT TO DO IF YOUR PARENT DOESN'T WANT TO TAKE MEDICINE

When faced with resistance or refusal from your aging parent regarding medication, it can be difficult to determine the best course of action. Below are four typical reasons why older adults may discontinue their medication, along with practical advice for addressing each issue.

Undesirable Taste

If your parent is reluctant to take their medication because of its taste, there are ways to address this issue. Check the prescription label to see if the medication can be taken with food. Mix or blend pills with food or place them in soft foods if you can. If the medication needs to be taken without food, give it to them with water. When considering food pairing, keep the following factors in mind:

- Is the medication to be taken on an empty stomach?
- Can the medication be crushed to help with swallowing or mixed with food?
- Is taking the medication with dairy products or specific juices safe?

Side Effects

Frequently, older adults decline medication due to troublesome side effects. Stronger medications may cause unwelcome side effects. Be mindful and inquire about your parent's experience. Discuss concerns with their healthcare provider or pharmacist for alternative therapies or guidance to alleviate symptoms and prevent further complications.

Forgetfulness

Forgetfulness can cause dementia patients to refuse medication, believing they've already taken it. This poses a serious risk for those living alone. Occasional forgetfulness is understandable, but recurring issues require proactive solutions. Caregiver advocacy is crucial for aging parents with medication management. Accompany them to doctor's visits, bring their meds, and ask questions for better care and medication adherence.

Here are some strategies to consider:

- **Pill organizers:** This helps organize medications by day and time, making it easier for your parents to keep track.
- **Medication management:** These devices dispense medication at set times and can be programmed to send reminders.
- **Reminder services:** Set alarms on your parents' phones to remind them to take their medication.
- **Reducing medications (with physician approval):** Speak to your parent's doctor about combining medications to reduce the number of needed pills.

Simply Not Caring

To handle an aging parent refusing medication, understand the root cause. Open conversations and consulting with doctors or pharmacists can help. Seek therapist support if needed. Always consult healthcare professionals for a safe and tailored care plan.

HEALTHCARE APPOINTMENTS

Accompanying your parents to a medical appointment can place you in various roles. Suddenly, you're not just a concerned family member but also a caregiver and a medical advocate. Our tips aim to assist you in navigating and supporting your parents in receiving the care they need.

Gather Before Medical Visits

Before your parent's medical appointment, taking a few direct steps is wise to ensure a smooth and productive visit. Here's what you can do:

- Call ahead to accompany your parent, ask if you can be in the exam room, and provide health care proxy documentation.
- Gather your parent's medical history, including current health conditions, past surgeries, medications, supplements, and medication allergies from family members if needed.
- Complete the necessary paperwork before your appointment to save time. Ask if it can be mailed or downloaded beforehand.
- Compile relevant information to discuss your parent's medication adherence, memory lapses, daily activities, mobility, and routines for the doctor's assessment.

The Day of the Medical Visit

Here's a checklist to help you prepare for your parent's medical appointment:

- **Make a list of concerns:** Create a brief list of your parent's symptoms, questions, and medical concerns for the doctor.
- **Bag up all medications:** Bring these to the appointment for a clear overview of your parent's medication to prevent errors and aid review.

- **Decide who's talking:** Discuss with your parent their comfort with the interaction during the appointment, respect their preferences, and be ready to jump in.
- **Be respectful of your parents:** Avoid treating them like children or criticizing them, especially in front of the doctor. Use kind and supportive language, helping them retain their dignity throughout the appointment.
- **Take notes:** Bring a notebook or use your phone to jot down the doctor's observations, advice, and instructions. Write down the answers to your concerns and questions for future reference.

After the Medical Visit

After the medical appointment, following up to ensure your parent receives the necessary care and stay informed about their health is important. Here's what you can do:

- **Post instructions:** If the doctor provides specific instructions, like medication changes or lifestyle recommendations, post them on the refrigerator or in your parent's home, where they can easily get to them.
- **Provide written notes:** Write or print out your notes from the appointment and give them to your parent for their records. This allows them to review the doctor's observations, advice, and instructions.
- **Ensure medication compliance:** Ensure your parent accepts any prescribed medications and understands how to take them correctly. If necessary, assist them

in organizing their medications using pill organizers or reminder systems.

- **Mark upcoming appointments:** Note any upcoming medical appointments or tests on your parent's calendar to help them stay organized and prepared. This ensures they attend important follow-up visits or screenings.

DEALING WITH ELDERLY PARENT'S DOCTOR APPOINTMENT REFUSAL

Caring for aging parents can be challenging, especially when it comes to getting them to their medical appointments. However, there are ways to encourage reluctant parents to prioritize these checkups. From gentle reminders to highlighting the benefits of regular medical care, you can break down resistance and encourage cooperation. With the right approach, we can ensure our aging parents receive the care they need and deserve. So, roll up your sleeves, tap into your creativity, and tackle this challenge together.

Investigate the Resistance

To convince your parents to visit the doctor, explain the purpose of the visits and how they can help monitor specific health conditions. You can also consider professional senior care to help them live better and healthier lives. Home care assistance provides support with daily tasks, illness prevention, and overall well-being, empowering them to thrive gracefully as they age.

Integrate Other Activities

Do you want to make those doctor trips more bearable for your parents? These little detours can turn a routine visit into a memorable adventure, easing apprehensions and making the experience more enjoyable for everyone involved. So, why not add excitement to their next doctor's appointment? Your parents will thank you, and you'll all walk away with smiles.

Here's a pro tip:

- Sprinkle in some fun before or after the appointment.
- Treat your parents to a delicious lunch.
- Go to the mall for a stroll.

Change the Routine

To help your parents attend medical appointments, involve a family member or hire hourly caregivers who can provide support and reassurance. These caregivers also offer companionship and transportation for daily errands. Home care professionals specialize in providing high-quality assistance to seniors, like mobility and exercise assistance, transportation to medical appointments, and social events. They help aging parents maintain their independence and well-being.

Coordinate Care

Consolidating your parents' appointments on the same day can be wise if they see multiple practitioners, as long as spending an extended period away from home is manageable. If you're dealing with a parent who consistently resists attending medical appointments, empathy is key. Take it from their point of view and understand their fears and concerns. Seniors must maintain good health, not skip regular checkups, or ignore emerging health issues.

MANAGING HOSPITAL STAYS

When your parent faces hospitalization, it can be an emotionally taxing and worrisome experience for everyone. The stress and uncertainty are natural, but with a strategic approach, you can offer support to facilitate their recovery and well-being. Here are some vital aspects to prioritize during this challenging time:

Communication Is Key

Effective communication is essential during a hospitalization. Setting open and transparent lines of communication with the healthcare team overseeing your parent's care is vital. Take steps to comprehend the specifics of their illness, the proposed treatment, and the anticipated timeline for recovery. Stay vigilant and ensure you're promptly notified of any changes in their condition. This proactive approach fosters transparency and collaboration, ultimately enhancing the quality of care your parents receive.

Be Actively Involved

Taking an active role in your parent's care can deliver significant benefits. Whenever possible, attend doctor's rounds to stay informed and engaged. Feel free to ask questions and offer insights into your parent's medical history, allergies, or any unique needs the hospital staff may need to know. Your firsthand knowledge and involvement can enhance the quality of care, ensuring that your parent receives personalized attention that aligns with their specific requirements and preferences.

Managing Medications

Hospitalizations frequently lead to medication alterations. It's vital to understand any new medications prescribed during this time comprehensively. Identify their purpose, potential side effects, and how they may interact with existing medications. This knowledge empowers you to advocate effectively for your parent's well-being and ensures their medication is optimized for safety and efficacy. Don't hesitate to consult with healthcare professionals to address any concerns or uncertainties regarding medication changes, as clear communication is key to promoting your parents' health and recovery.

Support Their Emotional Well-Being

Hospital stays can be very emotional for your aging parent, often producing feelings of fear, loneliness, and anxiety. Your presence, reassurance, and empathy can make a difference during this challenging time. You provide invaluable support and comfort by being there for them, alleviating their distress, and promoting security. Take the time to listen to their concerns, offer encouragement, and provide companionship to ease their emotional burden. Your unwavering support serves as a beacon of strength during their journey to recovery, reinforcing the bond of love and care between you and your parent.

Coordinate Post-Hospital Care

It's vital to have a well-defined plan in place for your parent's post-hospital care before they're discharged. This plan may include home care services, rehabilitation, or follow-up appointments. Discuss the details with the healthcare team to ensure clarity and address concerns. By understanding the post-hospital care plan entirely, you can efficiently coordinate and implement the necessary arrangements to support your parent's recovery and well-being as they transition back home.

Prepare Their Home for Recovery

Creating a supportive home environment is crucial for post-hospital care for your parent. Adjustments like installing grab bars and removing cluttered pathways can improve mobility. If they use a wheelchair, install ramps and widen doorways to accommodate their needs. These modifications promote safety and comfort for your loved one, enabling them to recover at home easily. By addressing these environmental considerations proactively, you can optimize the healing process and facilitate a smoother transition for your parent.

Understand Their Dietary Needs

Nutrition is a crucial component of the recovery process. Upon your parent's return home, consulting with the hospital nutritionist or dietitian can offer valuable insight into their dietary needs. It's vital to grasp any dietary restrictions or recommendations provided and plan meals accordingly. Understanding and sticking to these guidelines can help support your parent's recovery journey and promote optimal health and well-being. Feel free to seek clarification or additional guidance from healthcare professionals to ensure your parent receives the nutrition they need to thrive during their recovery.

GETTING SUPPORT FOR HEALTHCARE

Getting healthcare support for your aging parents is important for ensuring they receive the care they need as they grow older. This support can come in various forms, including government programs and nonprofit organizations that assist seniors with medical expenses. By exploring these resources, you can alleviate the financial burden of healthcare costs and ensure access to essential care for your aging parents.

Medicare

Medicare is a federal health insurance program primarily designed for individuals aged 65 and older and certain younger individuals with disabilities or specific medical conditions. It provides coverage for various healthcare services and expenses, helping to ensure access to essential medical care for eligible beneficiaries.

Medicare plays a critical role in providing healthcare coverage for your parents, helping to ensure access to medical services, and promoting overall well-being during retirement years.

Here are some key points about Medicare for your aging parents:

- **Coverage:** Medicare consists of several parts, each covering different aspects of healthcare:
- **Hospital:** Hospital insurance that helps cover inpatient hospital stays, skilled nursing facility care, hospice care, and some home health care.
- **Medical:** Medical insurance helps cover doctor's services, outpatient care, medical supplies, and preventive services.
- **Private:** Private insurance companies approved by Medicare typically include coverage for Parts A and B and often prescription drug coverage (Part D), along with additional benefits.
- **Enrollment:** Most seniors become eligible for Medicare when they turn 65, although eligibility criteria may vary based on specific circumstances. Enrollment typically occurs during an initial enrollment period around the time of eligibility, with additional opportunities for enrollment during specified periods.

- **Costs:** While many Medicare services are provided at no cost to beneficiaries, certain expenses, like premiums, deductibles, coinsurance, and copayments, may apply, depending on the type of coverage and services received. Medicare Advantage and Part D plans offered by private insurance companies may have additional costs and coverage options.
- **Coverage limitations:** While Medicare provides comprehensive coverage for many healthcare services, it does not cover all medical expenses. For example, it may not cover certain dental, vision, hearing, or long-term care services. Supplementary insurance plans, such as Medigap policies, can help fill gaps in coverage.

Medicaid

Medicaid is a government program that provides healthcare coverage to low-income individuals. It's the largest insurance provider in the United States, covering over 70 million Americans. Medicaid ensures access to essential healthcare services, including doctor's visits, hospital stays, and prescription drugs. It's an indispensable resource for promoting equitable healthcare access and addressing disparities.

Long-Term Care Insurance

Life and long-term care insurance are essential for managing healthcare and personal care costs in retirement. Life insurance holders offer policies with a long-term care component, providing seniors with funds for in-home care and other expenses. By incorporating long-term care coverage within life insurance, seniors can have financial protection and peace of mind. These options safeguard seniors' financial well-being and ensure they receive the necessary care and support to enjoy a comfortable retirement.

Asset Protection Trusts

An irrevocable trust can safeguard assets without affecting Medicaid eligibility. Assets are transferred to a trustee, removing them from the individual's control. Once established, the trust can't be altered or dissolved without beneficiaries' consent. Revocable trusts allow modification but don't assist in Medicaid qualification. An irrevocable trust provides asset protection while potentially qualifying for Medicaid benefits, making it a valuable tool for long-term financial planning.

Gifting Assets Before Eldercare

Gifting assets to aging parents can be thoughtful, but it's important to consider the implications and potential consequences. While gifting assets to parents can be a meaningful way to provide support, it's essential to approach the decision thoughtfully and consider the potential implications and consequences. Consulting with professionals can help ensure that any gifts best serve your parents' long-term interests and financial well-being.

Here are some key points to keep in mind:

- **Medicaid eligibility:** Gifting assets to aging parents may impact Medicaid eligibility for long-term care due to strict asset transfer rules.
- **Tax implications:** Before making any decisions, a tax advisor or financial planner should discuss the tax implications of large gifts.
- **Financial stability:** Consider your parent's financial situation and whether gifting assets could impact their financial stability or ability to meet their ongoing expenses and healthcare needs.
- **Estate planning:** It's important to discuss potential gifts with your parents and their estate planning attorney to align with their goals.
- **Legal and financial advice:** Before proceeding with asset transfers, seek legal and financial professionals specializing in elder law and estate planning.

In Chapter 6, we delved into the numerous government and nonprofit programs aimed at helping individuals manage medical expenses and access essential care.

Moving into Chapter 7, "Build Your Caregiver Network," we'll focus on establishing a robust support system and strategies for building that network.

7

BUILD YOUR CAREGIVER NETWORK

During our first few weeks and months as caregivers, Sam and I realized the importance of daily routines. I cannot stress enough the importance of establishing a daily routine. Write down on paper every single thing you do and what time you do it from the first minute of the morning through the last minute of the evening. Add items to the list as you do them. Your list will be long.... multiple pages long... do it anyway.

It is important to do this for various reasons, but mostly so you can repeat it the same way every day. Your parents' care will be much easier to manage when you can check items off the list as they are accomplished during the day, and your parents know what to expect next. This is also a huge help when you need someone to occasionally step in and relieve you.

The idea of helping a full-time caregiver get a little respite isn't quite so intimidating if you have a step-by-step written routine for them to follow. Lastly, this all-inclusive list validates the exceptional care you are giving your parents. Remember, your family and friends who are not living inside the home don't see everything you do. They do not realize the effort you are putting into the care and concern you have for your parents.

Our family has always been very involved in our church and local community. Kay and Mike were the behind-the-scenes workers at church, always cleaning and repairing as they saw the needs arise. They rarely asked for help and never asked for compensation. They also volunteered at the local food and clothing bank. Always having a heart to serve others first, Mike was well known as a Prayer Warrior. When someone expressed a need, Mike was faithful in writing their name down on his prayer list and would faithfully pray until he saw that person again. He would ask how that particular situation was working out. He would continue to pray until he knew that prayer had been answered. Through their faithfulness in serving, Kay and Mike were known throughout our community and loved by so many. It was not difficult for Sam and me to find willing volunteers to come for a visit and relieve us of our caregiving responsibilities from time to time. The step-by-step routine I printed out was an immeasurable help to everyone who offered to relieve us.

Sam's siblings came to relieve us for an entire week during our summer vacation. They were so thankful for the step-by-step instructions I printed out because they could step right in without disrupting Kay and Mike's daily routine. This also allowed them more quality time visiting rather than trying to figure things out. It also opened their eyes to what being a caregiver involves. By the end of our vacation week, Sam's siblings were thankful for the list because they could spend quality time with their parents and were thankful for what they knew we were doing on behalf of their parents.

YOUR CAREGIVING NETWORK

Building a caregiver network is essential for effective care and support for aging parents or loved ones. This network consists of various individuals and resources that offer assistance, guidance, and encouragement throughout the caregiving journey. From family members and friends to healthcare professionals and community organizations, each member plays a crucial role in providing holistic care and alleviating the challenges of caregiving.

In this chapter, we will explore the importance of building a robust caregiver network and provide practical tips for connecting with and leveraging the support of those around you. Strengthening your caregiver network can ensure you have the necessary resources and support to navigate the complexities of caregiving with confidence and compassion.

FAMILY AND FRIENDS

Caregivers need emotional support, practical assistance, and companionship throughout their journey. Family and friends form the cornerstone of their support system. By building strong relationships, caregivers can share responsibilities, get an ear to listen, and find respite care to ensure the best possible care for their loved ones. This support system can significantly affect the well-being of the caregiver and the aging parent. Let's explore how to cultivate and leverage these relationships to help caregivers receive the support they need.

Communicate Your Needs

Communicating your needs is fundamental to building a solid caregiver network. You can effectively enlist support from family members, friends, and other caregivers by openly expressing your challenges, concerns, and requirements. Here are some tips for communicating your needs effectively:

- **Be honest:** Share your feelings and experiences openly and honestly with your loved ones.
- **Be specific:** Whether you need help with daily tasks, emotional support, or respite care, provide specific details to help others understand how they can best support you.
- **Set boundaries:** Establish clear boundaries regarding the type and extent of assistance you need.
- **Use "I" statements:** Frame your needs using "I" statements to express your thoughts and feelings without sounding accusatory.
- **Provide updates:** Communicate regularly to help maintain transparency and ensure everyone remains on the same page.
- **Seek solutions together:** Encourage open dialogue and explore different strategies for effectively addressing your needs.

- **Express gratitude:** Express gratitude to strengthen your relationships and encourage continued assistance from your caregiver network.

WHEN FAMILY SUPPORT FALLS SHORT

When family support falls short, caregivers face challenges and are overwhelmed. Not all relatives offer the assistance they need for various reasons. Coping strategies include:

- **Acknowledge feelings:** Address disappointment or frustration when support is lacking.
- **Have realistic expectations:** Recognize each member's limitations and responsibilities.
- **Seek understanding:** Understand reasons for the lack of support, such as distance or obligations.
- **Have open conversations:** Discuss caregiving needs openly and respectfully with family.
- **Identify alternatives:** Explore other support sources like friends, support groups, or professional caregivers.
- **Set boundaries:** Protect well-being by setting clear limits on additional responsibilities.
- **Practice self-care:** Prioritize personal well-being with activities that bring joy and relaxation.
- **Seek professional help:** Consider therapy or support groups for guidance and coping strategies.

Remember, asking for help is okay, even if it's not from immediate family. By proactively addressing the situation, caregivers can manage responsibilities and maintain well-being.

COMMUNITY SERVICES

Specialized programs and community services can help older adults with disabilities maintain their independence and quality of life at home. However, not all local areas can access these programs despite their nationwide availability. Several community services can provide support in caring for your aging parent.

Types of Community Services

Community services for seniors are tailored to meet various needs and preferences. These services typically include:

- **Healthcare services:** Access to medical professionals, including doctors, nurses, and specialists, for routine checkups, consultations, and specialized care.
- **Home care assistance:** In-home caregivers aid with daily tasks such as bathing, dressing, meal prep, medication management, and light housekeeping.
- **Transportation assistance:** Rides for seniors to medical appointments, grocery stores, pharmacies, and social outings when driving is not an option.
- **Nutrition programs:** Meal delivery, congregate meal sites, and nutrition counseling ensure access to healthy food options and promote good eating habits.
- **Social and recreational activities:** Senior centers and adult day programs offer socialization, education, exercise, and leisure activities for overall well-being.

- **Financial and legal assistance:** Counseling and services help with financial planning, benefits enrollment, estate management, and legal matters.
- **Respite care:** Temporary care services give family caregivers breaks while their aging parents receive care.
- **Housing options:** Affordable housing tailored to seniors' needs, such as independent living, assisted living, and nursing homes.
- **Support groups and counseling:** Peer support and counseling aid seniors in managing transitions, chronic conditions, and emotional concerns.
- **Volunteer programs:** Opportunities for seniors to engage in meaningful projects and contribute to their communities through volunteering.

These community services support seniors' health, independence, and overall well-being, allowing them to age with dignity and thrive in their preferred living environment.

Empowering, Supportive Communities

- Supportive communities encompass various social networks and organizations.
- They provide assistance, resources, and support to individuals facing challenges.
- Types of supportive communities include local or online support groups, nonprofits, and religious congregations.
- These communities offer emotional support, practical assistance, and valuable resources.

- Members share common experiences, interests, and goals, fostering connections.
- Supportive communities empower members to collaborate, learn, and grow together.
- They advocate for positive social change and address community needs effectively.
- These communities promote inclusivity, diversity, and mutual respect.
- They play a crucial role in fostering resilience, connection, and empowerment.

GERIATRIC CARE MANAGERS

Geriatric care managers, also known as elder or senior care managers, are licensed professionals, typically nurses, social workers, or gerontologists, specializing in senior care management. Serving as a "professional relative," they offer impartial guidance and support, guiding families through challenging and emotionally charged discussions.

These professionals assist families and seniors in identifying areas of concern and collaboratively developing personalized senior care plans. These plans address seniors' needs while providing peace of mind for family members and caregivers.

When Do You Need One?

You may benefit from the expertise of a senior care manager in various situations, including:

- **Complex care needs:** When multiple health issues require coordination among healthcare providers or assistance managing medications
- **Family disagreements:** In cases of differing opinions on care decisions or communication challenges among family members
- **Long-distance caregiving:** When overseeing care from afar and needing regular updates on aging parents' well-being
- **Transitioning care:** During moves between care settings, such as hospitals, homes, or assisted living facilities
- **Navigating resources:** For guidance on resources like home care agencies, support groups, or financial assistance programs
- **End-of-life planning:** When making decisions about hospice or palliative care, ensure the senior's wishes are respected with support from a care manager

Overall, a geriatric care manager can provide invaluable support in navigating the complexities of senior care, offering expertise, guidance, and peace of mind for seniors and their families.

HIRING A CARE MANAGER

Geriatric care managers, elder care managers, or aging life care professionals play a vital role in assisting families with challenging decisions regarding senior care.

Before hiring a geriatric care manager, consider the following factors:

- **Background and training:** Ensure they have relevant experience and qualifications in senior care.
- **Certifications:** Look for certifications like CGCM or CCM, indicating professionalism and expertise.
- **Costs:** Clarify fees and payment structure, including services covered and additional charges.
- **References and reviews:** Seek feedback from past clients and professionals to assess reputation.
- **Communication and collaboration:** Evaluate their communication skills and ability to collaborate with seniors, families, and healthcare providers.
- **Compatibility:** Ensure a good fit between the care manager and your loved one for effective advocacy and support.

By carefully considering these factors, you can make an informed decision when hiring a geriatric care manager who will provide high-quality care and support for your loved one.

Questions to Ask Your Geriatric Care Manager

When hiring a geriatric care manager, asking specific questions is important to ensure they fit your loved one's needs. Here are some key questions to consider:

- **Background and experience:** What's your experience in geriatric care management, particularly with clients similar to my loved ones?
- **Certifications and credentials:** Do you hold geriatric care management certifications, and are you a member of relevant professional organizations?

- **Services and approach:** What services do you provide as a geriatric care manager, and how do you assess needs and develop care plans while involving seniors and their families?
- **Costs and fees:** What are your fees and fee structure for geriatric care management services, including any additional costs?
- **References and testimonials:** Do you have references or testimonials from past clients or healthcare professionals?
- **Communication and collaboration:** How do you communicate with clients and families, including when you are available for updates and consultations? How do you collaborate with other healthcare providers?
- **Emergency and crisis management:** What's your approach to handling emergencies or crises with your loved one and ensuring continuity of care?
- **Ethical considerations:** How do you prioritize confidentiality and privacy for clients, and how do you handle conflicts of interest or ethical dilemmas?

By asking these questions, you can gain valuable insight into the geriatric care manager's qualifications, services, and approach, helping you make an informed decision about their suitability for your loved one's care needs.

IN-HOME CARE

Caring for someone around the clock while working full-time and providing long-distance care can be challenging. Hiring help can alleviate burdens, allowing you to prioritize self-care. Trusted assistance can handle errands and house-hold chores, relieving caregivers of demanding schedules. Involving another caregiver can lead to smoother coopera-tion from the care recipient and help maintain a positive relationship dynamic. With support, you can better manage your caregiving responsibilities while finding time to recharge and engage in activities that bring you joy.

My Loved One Only Wants Me to Help

Helping your parents accept assistance can be challenging, but your presence can help. Demonstrate how you handle tasks to make the assistance feel familiar and comfortable. Emphasize that you need help and hiring assistance supports you in caring for them. Assure them that hiring help doesn't mean abandoning them. If they resist, suggest a trial period and consider an attendant with a similar background. Presenting the attendant as a "housekeeper" for household tasks initially can help ease them into accepting assistance with personal care.

How Do I Find Help?

There are two methods for finding an attendant:

- formal
- informal

When searching for a home care agency, seek advice from your doctor, friends, or local community members. Numerous agencies are available in urban and suburban areas, while options may be more limited in rural areas.

Check online reviews and contact your local Area Agency on Aging for recommendations.

When contacting agencies, ask essential questions such as:

- Does the state license the agency?
- How long has the agency been in operation?
- Are the workers licensed and insured?
- What training, supervision, and monitoring processes does the agency have for its workers?

Requesting a packet of information from the agency detailing their services, fees, and references allows you to review the information beforehand and prepare for a face-to-face meeting with a representative.

Home Care Agency Pros and Cons

Pros of hiring through an agency:

- The agency manages screening, hiring/firing, pay, and taxes.
- Some agencies offer attendants with various skills and can match you with a staff member who can provide the necessary care.
- They can accommodate variable schedules and provide substitutes if the assigned worker is unavailable.
- Agencies can assist in settling disputes and are often covered by long-term care insurance.

Cons of hiring through an agency:

- They may schedule multiple attendants if work hours are inconsistent, requiring adjustment for each new person.
- Higher turnover rates among staff may occur.
- Certain tasks may be limited or charged at a higher rate.
- They are typically more expensive than private hire.

Private Hire Pros and Cons

Pros of hiring privately:

- You can choose the person you want from a screened pool and are in control as the employer.
- There's more flexibility in the tasks that can be performed.
- Typically, it is less expensive than hiring through an agency.
- It offers the opportunity to build a long-term relationship with the attendant(s).

Cons of hiring privately:

- If the worker is sick, you must find alternate help.
- You are responsible for all aspects of employment, including hiring/firing, payroll, taxes, insurance, and resolving employee disputes.
- Long-term care insurance may not be covered.

To hire a personal attendant, you can find someone privately via word of mouth, in organizations, or online. It requires you to handle all aspects of being an employer, including conducting background checks and verifying credentials.

Key Questions to Ask When Hiring Privately

- What are the aide's credentials, and can they be verified?
- Where has the aide worked previously, and can you provide references?
- Is the aide legally eligible to work in this country, and can they provide documentation?

What Will It Cost?

The rules and regulations for hired help vary significantly from state to state and even within cities. To ensure compliance, start by checking with your state's Department of Labor and familiarize yourself with the regulations in the specific municipality where the care will be provided.

Here are some key considerations:

- **Minimum wage:** Find out the minimum wage in your area, as this will determine the baseline for compensation.
- **Hours of work:** Determine the number of help you require. Some states require overtime pay and minimum uninterrupted sleep hours for live-in help.
- **Payroll setup:** If you hire privately, set up a payroll system. Some may prefer 1099 payment, so ensure they meet local requirements.

- **Payment method:** Some attendants may prefer cash payments. Clarify payment preferences and ensure compliance with local regulations.

If you hire through a home care agency:

- **Pay rate:** The agency will establish the pay rate, which may vary depending on the type of care needed.
- **Minimum hours:** Agencies may have minimum hour requirements for shifts.
- **Shift options:** Depending on the level of care needed, options may include full-time live-in care, live-in with additional awake hours, multiple shifts, etc.

Other considerations:

- **Vacation pay:** Decide whether you'll compensate the attendant during your vacations.
- **Holiday gifts/bonuses:** Consider whether you'll provide monetary or physical gifts during holidays and whether yearly bonuses are expected.
- **Severance pay:** Determine if severance pay is appropriate for termination without cause.

These decisions should be considered to avoid confusion or burden when needed.

How Can I Afford It?

Hiring in-home help can be a significant expense, especially for full-time care. However, the cost can be more manageable if you require only a few hours of assistance each week. Hourly rates vary depending on your location in the United States.

Here are some ways to offset the cost:

- **Long-term care insurance:** Check the policy for coverage eligibility and details.
- **Tax deductions:** Consult a tax accountant about possible deductions for medically necessary hired help.
- **Medicaid:** In-home support services are available through Medicaid for low-income individuals. Contact the local office for details.
- **Personal savings:** Use savings or family contributions to cover expenses.
- **Community resources:** Some communities offer low-cost home care options. Contact local agencies for details.
- **Senior service agencies:** Seek assistance finding lower-cost attendant care.

Exploring these options can help alleviate the financial burden of in-home care while ensuring your loved one receives the support they need.

HOW DO I FIND THE RIGHT PERSON?

When hiring help, it's crucial to outline the specific tasks you need assistance with. Drafting a detailed job description ensures clear communication and mutual understanding. Here's how to create an effective job description:

- **Specific duties:** List housekeeping tasks and preferences, like laundry preferences.
- **Personal care needs:** Outline assistance with dressing, grooming, and toileting.
- **Companion responsibilities:** Describe preferences for activities and companionship.
- **Pet care:** Specify pet-related tasks and check for allergies.
- **Experience with dementia:** Inquire about experience with cognitive impairment.
- **Certifications:** Home care attendants like HHAs, CNAs, or LVNs may hold certifications. Legal duties vary by state, so clarify requirements with candidates.

By detailing your needs and expectations upfront, you can ensure that you and the attendant are on the same page regarding care responsibilities and standards.

Checking References

Verifying references and conducting background checks before hiring an attendant is important. References provide insight into the candidate's past performance and reliability. Contact previous employers or clients to inquire about the candidate's work ethic and communication skills. Background checks help ensure safety and security by uncovering criminal history and verifying identity. By diligently checking references and conducting background checks, you can make informed hiring decisions and ensure the well-being of your loved one.

Write a Job Description

When crafting a job description for a caregiver, it's essential to be thorough and specific about the tasks involved and any requirements or preferences you have. Here's a template to guide you:

Job Title

In-Home Caregiver

Job Description

We seek a compassionate and experienced caregiver to provide in-home assistance to [*Name of Care Receiver*]. The caregiver will be responsible for [list specific tasks like personal care, household chores, companionship, etc.]. Additionally, the caregiver should be proficient in [mention any specific skills or certifications required].

Responsibilities

- Assist with activities of daily living, including bathing, dressing, grooming, toileting, and transferring.
- Perform household chores like cooking, cleaning, laundry, and grocery shopping.

- Engage in meaningful activities and companionship with the care receiver.
- Monitor and administer medications as prescribed by healthcare professionals.
- Assist with mobility and transfers, including mobility aids or Hoyer lift if necessary.
- Provide support and supervision for individuals with memory or cognitive impairments.
- Communicate effectively with the care receiver, family members, and healthcare professionals.
- Drive care receiver to appointments or outings as needed.
- Provide care for pets, including feeding, walking, and grooming.

Requirements

- certification as a CNA, LVN, or HHA preferred
- experience working with individuals with memory or cognitive impairments
- valid driver's license and clean driving record (if driving is required)
- ability to lift and transfer care receiver safely
- excellent communication and interpersonal skills
- fluency in [mention any specific languages required]
- non-smoker (if applicable)
- flexible hours or days required

Additional Information (If Hiring Privately)

- **Compensation:** Mention the hourly rate or payment terms.

- **Benefits:** Mention the benefits, such as holiday pay, vacation/sick leave, etc.
- **Payment method:** Specify whether payment will be made in cash, check, or through payroll services.
- **Meal arrangements:** Specify if meals will be provided or if the caregiver needs to bring their food.

You can attract qualified candidates who meet your needs and preferences by providing a detailed job description.

Interviewing

When hiring through an agency, the process is streamlined, saving you time and effort. Agencies typically conduct initial interviews over the phone and provide resumes and references for potential candidates. Once you've identified suitable applicants, you can arrange an in-person interview at your loved one's home or nearby.

Here's a step-by-step guide for interviewing potential caregivers:

- **Phone screening:** Conduct initial phone interviews to discuss interests and qualifications.
- **In-person interview:** Schedule in-person meetings involving the care receiver if possible.
- **Interview questions:** Ask relevant questions based on the job description.
- **Observation:** Observe candidate interactions with the care receiver.

- **References:** Contact the provided references for verification.
- **Impressions:** Consider feedback from involved parties and trust instincts.
- **Job offer:** Extend offers promptly to prevent losing candidates.
- **Contract signing:** Arrange contract signings and establish start dates.

Following these steps, you can efficiently hire a qualified caregiver through an agency and ensure a smooth transition for your loved one's care.

WRITING A CONTRACT FOR HIRING HELP

When hiring a caregiver privately, it's important to establish a formal contract to clarify expectations and responsibilities for both parties. Here's a checklist for developing a contract:

Employer: [Your Name]

Employee: [Attendant's Name]

Contact Information:

Employer Address: [Your Address]

Employee Address: [Attendant's Address]

Employer Phone: [Your Phone Number]

Employee Phone: [Attendant's Phone Number]

Employer Social Security Number: [Your SSN]

Employee Social Security Number: [Attendant's SSN]

- **Wages:** Specify agreed-upon wages and reimbursement details. Request a copy of the driver's license and car insurance if applicable.
- **Paperwork:** Determine how to maintain paperwork, like daily logs or medication lists. Clarify record-keeping expectations.
- **Behavior expectations:** Outline behavior expectations, including phone use, smoking policies, and punctuality.
- **Termination clause:** Define grounds for termination, notice requirements, and whether termination requires cause.
- **Date and signatures:** Include a section for both parties to date and sign the contract, indicating agreement.
- **Legal consultation:** Consider legal advice to ensure compliance with employment laws and regulations.

By understanding and fulfilling your legal and financial responsibilities as an employer, you can ensure compliance with regulations and maintain a positive working relationship with your household employee.

COMMUNICATION

Effective caregiving requires open communication between you, the caregiver, and the care receiver. Schedule regular meetings to discuss any concerns, changes in care needs, or household dynamics. Be clear about expectations and provide adequate training. Build trust through transparent communication and mutual respect. Show appreciation for a job well done. Finding the right caregiver is invaluable—best of luck on your caregiving journey.

In this chapter, we've explored the complexities of hiring in-home help for caregiving, from determining your needs to navigating the hiring process through agencies or privately. We've highlighted the importance of clear communication, establishing expectations, and fostering trusting relationships with caregivers.

As we move into Chapter 8, we'll delve into the delicate balance of managing career and family life while fulfilling caregiving responsibilities. Join us as we uncover strategies to maintain equilibrium amidst these demanding roles, offering practical insights and empowering solutions to help you navigate this challenging terrain with confidence and resilience. Get ready to embark on a journey toward achieving harmony in your multifaceted life as a caregiver, family member, and professional.

8

BALANCE CAREER AND FAMILY
LIFE WITH CAREGIVING

During Sam's childhood, his parents were very involved in their local church. It was a small chapel where attendees were more like family members. Because Mike and Kay lived on a small lakefront in Florida, most chapel baptisms took place at their home.

Mike and Kay were excellent hosts who looked forward to opening their home to a gathering of friends and family where they would fellowship and celebrate special occasions. The love of entertaining friends and family in their house didn't fade as they aged.

When the time came that Mike and Kay were no longer physically able to leave their home and needed constant supervision, Sam and I realized we had a network of family and friends who felt comfortable coming for a "visit." These visits benefited all four of us once or twice a week. Mike and Kay could remain social despite physical limitations, and Sam and I could take short caregiving breaks.

Sam and I usually plan for a "guest" to come into the house on Fridays. We were careful not to call them "sitters." I would be sure to prepare some snacks in advance, so Kay would feel like she was entertaining her guests. She couldn't physically get up and serve anything, but I placed everything where the guests could self-serve.

We soon found that our network of friends and family genuinely enjoyed sitting with Mike and Kay for those short spells. They understood the importance of ministering to the needs of all of us. Mike and Kay needed interaction from friends and family outside our immediate household, and Sam and I needed time to do things as a couple.

Planning time for short breaks allows everyone an opportunity to hit the reset button. Due to Sam's siblings living several states away, they could not always help with the regular daily or weekly care schedules. Planning allowed Sam and I to schedule a few weekend getaways while his siblings spent quality time with their parents.

Sometimes, friends and family were unavailable to visit, and we needed someone to be home with Mike and Kay. We found that there are CNAs who will sit at an hourly rate. Contact your primary care physician or home health care Agencies for possible referrals.

BALANCING WORK WITH CAREGIVING

Balancing your responsibilities when nurturing your career and looking after your aging parents can be challenging. This section uncovers practical strategies tailored to the unique circumstances of balancing career aspirations with caregiving obligations. From mastering time management techniques and negotiating flexible work arrangements to nurturing open lines of communication with employers and family members, you need tools and insights to thrive in both realms.

As you are on your caregiving journey, you must celebrate the small victories, acknowledge the challenges, and remember the importance of self-care amidst personal and professional pursuits. Not everyone can solely focus on looking after their parents as they need to work. Finding a balance between these demands can be emotionally taxing and complex.

This chapter delves into effective strategies for gracefully and resiliently navigating this intricate terrain. It will explore the importance of open communication with your employer, advocating for flexibility, and understanding your caregiving responsibilities.

Additionally, we'll highlight the importance of prioritizing self-care and acknowledging that maintaining your well-being is important for providing quality care to your parents. We'll also discuss the necessity of having backup plans to ensure continuity of care during unexpected circumstances.

Balancing work and caring for aging parents can sometimes feel like you are walking a tightrope, but it is doable. Here are some steps you can take:

- **Talk to your employer:** Start a conversation with your employer to discuss your caregiving responsibilities. Explain the situation honestly and emphasize your commitment to your job. Explore potential accommodations like flexible hours, remote work options, or adjusted deadlines to better balance your work and caregiving duties. Keep the lines of communication open and be willing to negotiate mutually beneficial solutions.

- **Have a backup plan:** Develop a contingency plan for any unexpected emergencies or situations that may arise while you are at work. Identify trusted family members, friends, or professional caregivers who can care for your aging parents when needed. Ensure that everyone involved knows the backup plan and has access to important contact information and instructions.

- **Create time for yourself:** Prioritize self-care by carving out small pocket time each day. Use this time to participate in activities that bring you joy and help you relax. That could be reading a book, walking, working in the garden, or practicing mindfulness exercises. Remember that caring for yourself is vital for maintaining your well-being and resilience as a caregiver.

- **Adhere to safety measures and precautions:** Stay informed about health guidelines and recommendations from reputable sources like the CDC or WHO. Implement hygiene practices like frequent handwashing, wearing masks, and sanitizing high-touch surfaces in your home. Encourage your aging parents to follow safety protocols and minimize their risk of exposure to illness.

- **Draft a work-caregiving schedule:** Create a structured schedule that balances your work commitments with your caregiving responsibilities. Give yourself specific blocks of time for work tasks, caregiving duties, and personal activities. Be realistic about what you can accomplish every day. Prioritize your daily tasks based on their importance and urgency. Regularly review and adjust your schedule to adequately address work and caregiving duties.
- **Build a support team:** Enlist the support of family members, friends, and community resources to share the caregiving load. Delegate tasks and responsibilities to others and openly communicate your needs and limitations. Consider joining a local or online support group for caregivers to connect with people experiencing similar challenges and share advice and encouragement.
- **Make a task list:** Create a comprehensive list outlining your caregiving responsibilities, household chores, and work-related tasks. Break down any of your larger tasks into smaller, more manageable steps. Remember to always prioritize your tasks based on urgency and importance. Regularly check and update your task list to ensure everything runs smoothly.
- **Have a plan if you're working full time:** Develop a plan for managing your caregiving responsibilities while working full time. Explore flexible work arrangements with your employer, like telecommuting or adjusted hours, to accommodate your caregiving duties. Set boundaries between work and personal life, and prioritize self-care to prevent

burnout. Being transparent with your employer and colleagues about your current needs and limitations is essential. Seek support from community resources and loved ones when necessary.

BALANCING FAMILY LIFE AND CAREGIVING

Finding a healthy balance between your family life and caregiving is a journey of challenges and rewards. This section explores practical strategies and heartfelt insights to help you navigate this delicate balance with grace and resilience. From effective communication with your loved ones to prioritizing self-care and creating support networks, let's explore actionable steps to harmonize your caregiving responsibilities with the joys of family life.

Create a "Family Council"

Establishing a family council can foster unity, cohesion, and efficiency within your family dynamic, particularly when managing caregiving responsibilities. By creating a structured platform for open communication and collaboration, family members can collectively come together to address unique needs and challenges associated with caregiving.

This council can serve as a forum where all voices within your family are heard. It is a place where opinions should be valued, and decisions are made collaboratively, leading to a stronger sense of unity and shared purpose among family members.

Moreover, by centralizing discussions and decision-making processes related to caregiving, the family council helps streamline communication. It ensures everyone is on the same page regarding responsibilities, tasks, and expectations.

Establishing a family council can significantly enhance the efficiency and effectiveness of caregiving efforts, resulting in improved outcomes and a more harmonious family dynamic. Here's how to create one:

- **Define your objectives:** Clearly outline the purpose of the family council, like discussing caregiving needs, coordinating tasks, and ensuring everyone's well-being. Establish goals to guide your discussions and decision-making processes.
- **Choose council members:** Select family members directly involved in caregiving or impacted by responsibilities. Include your parents, siblings, spouses, and relevant individuals who can contribute to discussions and decision-making.
- **Set clear rules:** Establish participation, confidentiality, and decision-making guidelines within the family council. Encourage open communication, active listening, and respect for differing viewpoints. Ensure everyone has an opportunity to voice their opinions and concerns.
- **Schedule your meetings:** Set regular meeting times that accommodate everyone's schedules. If necessary, utilize technology for virtual meetings. Stick to the schedule to maintain consistency and accountability.
- **Allocate tasks:** Assign specific responsibilities and tasks to each family member based on strengths, availability, and preferences. Clearly define expectations and deadlines for completing tasks

related to caregiving, household chores, and other relevant areas.

By implementing these steps, you can create a collaborative and supportive environment within your family, ensuring effective communication and coordination in managing caregiving responsibilities.

Create a Family Calendar

Managing time efficiently is vital in the hustle and bustle of daily life, especially when juggling family commitments and caregiving responsibilities. One effective tool for achieving this balance is creating a family calendar.

It is important to have a calendar system that works for everyone within your family unit. Make sure to keep it updated and accessible to all family members. By creating a family calendar, you are taking control and steps to manage your time better and enhance harmony within your household.

To create a family calendar for efficient time management, follow these steps:

1. **Choose your calendar:** Select a calendar system that suits your family's preferences and needs. Options include digital calendars like Google Calendar, Apple Calendar, or Microsoft Outlook or a physical calendar placed in a central location in your home.
2. **Identify your daily activities:** List each family member's daily activities and commitments, including work schedules, school schedules,

extracurricular activities, appointments, and other obligations.

3. **Make a list of daily tasks:** Compile a list of daily tasks that need to be completed, including household chores, caregiving responsibilities, and tasks involving the person being cared for. Assign specific tasks to each family member based on their availability and capabilities.

4. **Keep your calendar updated:** Update the family calendar regularly with new events, appointments, and tasks as they arise. Encourage all family members to communicate any changes or additions to their schedules to ensure accuracy and prevent conflicts.

5. **Make sure the calendar is visible and accessible to everyone:** Place the family calendar in a prominent location in your home where everyone can easily see it, such as the kitchen or living room. Alternatively, share access to the digital calendar with all family members and encourage them to check it regularly.

Creating and maintaining a family calendar allows you to coordinate schedules, prioritize tasks, and ensure everyone is on the same page. This can help reduce stress, avoid conflicts, and improve overall time management for the entire family.

WORK AND LEISURE TRAVELS: WHAT TO DO WHEN YOU CAN'T BE THERE

Navigating the complexities of caregiving becomes even more challenging when work or leisure travels take you away. You always want to ensure your loved one is cared for, even when you cannot physically be there.

The great news is that you can still care for your parents even from a distance by delegating tasks, arranging alternative living arrangements, and using technology. Remember that where there is a plan, there is a way.

Here are some ideas about what you can do to make sure your parents are taken care of when you are away:

- **Evaluate what you can do:** Assess your caregiving responsibilities and determine what tasks can be managed remotely or delegated to others. Utilize technology to stay connected and monitor your loved one's well-being from a distance.
- **Explore different living arrangements:** Consider alternative living arrangements like assisted living facilities or in-home caregivers that can provide support in your absence. Research options to ensure your loved one receives appropriate care and assistance.
- **Have a family meeting:** Gather family members to discuss caregiving needs and develop a plan for when you're away. Assign responsibilities, establish communication channels, and ensure everyone knows their roles and obligations.
- **Plan visits:** Schedule regular visits by another family member or close friend with your loved one to maintain connection and provide hands-on support when possible. Coordinate visits with family members or caregivers to ensure continuity of care and address immediate needs or concerns.

- **Have an emergency plan:** Prepare an emergency plan outlining procedures to follow in case of unexpected situations or medical emergencies. Share emergency contact information, medical directives, and important documents with relevant individuals to ensure prompt and effective response.
- **Stay connected:** Regularly communicate with your loved one through phone calls, video chats, or messaging apps. Stay informed about their well-being, medication schedules, and any changes in their condition. Provide emotional support and reassurance, even from a distance.

This chapter addressed balancing caregiving, work, and family life. It provided some helpful ideas to help you better manage your day-to-day life and responsibilities. Remember that while caregiving is not the easiest of tasks, you can find ways to help you cope.

Now, get ready to dive deeper into the crucial topic of self-care in Chapter 9: "Practice Self-Care as the Caregiver." In the next chapter, we'll explore actionable strategies and empowering insights to help you nurture your physical, emotional, and mental well-being as a caregiver. Join us as we embark on this journey of self-discovery and learn how to cultivate resilience and vitality while providing compassionate care to those we love.

9

PRACTICING SELF-CARE AS THE CAREGIVER

While we were well aware of the commitment and sacrifices we agreed to make when we started our caregiving journey, it was not all roses and sunshine. This journey had its fair share of difficulties and huge personal sacrifices.

Our caregiving journey had us losing our freedom to come and go as we pleased. It also meant that our decisions were no longer ours alone. We had to consider Mike and Kay in each choice we made. Our lives were put on hold, and we quickly realized that many of our goals and dreams would never come to fruition.

As Mike and Kay's need for care progressed, they recognized that what we did for them was truly beneficial. At times, they became stubborn and challenging to deal with. Their minds reverted to childlike behaviors, and sometimes, they were outright defiant.

Looking back, Sam and I can now laugh about some of the shenanigans they pulled, but at the time they were happening, we were sometimes at our wits' end! I could write another book about all the crazy issues and frustrations we experienced.

I'll never forget the time Kay calmly and matter-of-factly told me that she and Mike had decided it was time for us to leave and move back into our own house. I must mention that this was shortly after we discovered that she had given Mike her injection of insulin and the same day that she had fallen in the kitchen and gashed her head open from hitting the stove. While it was obvious that we couldn't leave them, at the time, they were unable to understand that.

We were tired, on the verge of burnout, and desperately trying to give our very best. Sam and I prayed a very specific prayer every day: "Lord, please give us the strength, compassion, energy, and endurance we need to lovingly provide the best care possible. Help us allow Mike and Kay to age safely and with dignity. Protect our hearts, minds, and health in the process." It wasn't until about a year ago that Sam and I realized our prayer had been answered exceedingly and abundantly more than we asked or imagined.

CAREGIVER BURNOUT

Burnout is a state of physical, emotional, and mental exhaustion that caregivers can experience. It results from dedicating time and energy to the health and safety of another person. Being a caregiver, especially for your parents, is an important role that means that while caring for others, you also need to care for yourself.

As you devote yourself to caregiving, your identity becomes intertwined with this role. The constant emotional, moral, physical, and mental demands of caregiving can blur the lines between your personal and caregiver identities, affecting how you interact with others.

You might also find yourself in a place where you feel powerless over your parents' finances, mobility, and health can be incredibly frustrating. Despite your best efforts, you may question your purpose and feel helpless in the face of your declining condition.

Caring for a parent whose condition deteriorates over time can be emotionally draining. You may feel unappreciated and unfulfilled despite your dedication and care, especially if your parent cannot express gratitude or affection.

Caregiver burnout can exacerbate resentment and frustration, particularly when faced with unreasonable demands from your parent. You may feel unfairly blamed for circumstances beyond your control and struggle to cope with their harshness or criticism.

It's essential to continually assess your well-being and capacity to handle caregiving's mental, emotional, financial, and physical challenges. Recognizing warning signs and seeking support can help you prevent burnout.

SIGNS OF CAREGIVER BURNOUT

Recognizing the signs of caregiver burnout is important for safeguarding your well-being while fulfilling the responsibilities of caring for a loved one. Taking care of your aging parents can be emotionally and physically demanding. It can lead to stress, exhaustion, and feelings of overwhelm.

By acknowledging the warning signs of burnout early on, you can take proactive steps to prioritize self-care and seek support when needed. Ignoring these signs can lead to further strain on your mental and physical health, ultimately impacting your ability to provide quality care to your loved one. Therefore, it's crucial to pay attention to your needs and emotions and promptly address any signs of burnout to ensure you and your loved one receive the best possible care. Here are some common indicators to watch for:

- **Physical exhaustion:** Physical exhaustion manifests as constantly tired, exhausted, or run down. Caregivers may notice changes in their sleep patterns, such as difficulty falling asleep or staying asleep, which can contribute to feelings of burnout.
- **Emotional exhaustion:** Emotional exhaustion involves feeling overwhelmed by caregiving responsibilities. Caregivers may experience irritability, mood swings, or heightened anxiety levels. They might find themselves easily frustrated, even over minor issues, and may struggle to regulate their emotions effectively.
- **Withdrawal from activities:** Burnout can lead to losing interest in once-enjoyed activities. Caregivers may withdraw from social interactions, hobbies, or leisure activities, preferring to isolate themselves or spend time alone rather than engage in previously pleasurable pursuits.

- **Neglecting personal needs:** Caregivers experiencing burnout often prioritize the needs of their loved ones over their well-being. They may neglect basic self-care practices such as eating regularly, exercising, or attending medical appointments. This neglect can lead to worsening physical and mental health.
- **Decreased empathy:** Burnout can diminish a caregiver's ability to empathize with the person they care for. They may feel emotionally detached or indifferent to their loved one's needs and feelings, which can strain their relationship and further exacerbate feelings of guilt and frustration.
- **Increased illness:** Chronic stress and burnout can weaken the immune system, making caregivers more susceptible to illness. They may experience frequent headaches, stomachaches, or other physical symptoms as a result of prolonged stress and exhaustion.
- **Difficulty concentrating:** Burnout-related stress can impair cognitive function, making it difficult for caregivers to concentrate, make decisions, or remember things. They may feel mentally foggy or find it challenging to focus on tasks related to caregiving and other aspects of life.
- **Increased substance use:** Some caregivers may turn to alcohol, tobacco, or other substances as a coping mechanism for managing stress and emotional distress. This reliance on substances can quickly escalate and lead to dependency, exacerbating existing issues and further impacting the caregiver's well-being.

- **Changes in behavior:** Burnout can manifest in changes in behavior, such as engaging in risky behaviors, experiencing anger outbursts, or displaying signs of depression. Caregivers may become more irritable or impatient, lash out at others, or withdraw from social interactions altogether.

- **Feeling hopeless or helpless:** Caregivers experiencing burnout may feel hopeless or helpless about their caregiving role. They may question the purpose of their efforts and feel overwhelmed by the challenges they face. These feelings can contribute to a deep sense of despair and can significantly impact the caregiver's mental and emotional well-being.

If you recognize these signs in yourself, it's essential to prioritize self-care and seek support from friends, family, or professional resources. Taking proactive steps to address caregiver burnout can help you maintain your well-being and continue providing quality care for your loved one.

Caring for a loved one is a noble and compassionate endeavor, but it can also be draining. Caregiver burnout, a state of chronic stress and exhaustion, is a common challenge faced by many people who provide care to family members.

Here are some actionable tips to help you regain balance, resilience, and well-being in your caregiving journey:

- **Ask for help:** Don't hesitate to contact family members, friends, or neighbors for assistance with caregiving tasks. Whether running errands, preparing meals, or providing respite care, many people are willing to lend a helping hand if you ask. Be specific about what you need and how others can support you.
- **Get support:** Seek emotional support from others who understand your caregiving challenges. Joining support groups, either in-person or online, allows you to connect with fellow caregivers, share experiences, and receive empathy and encouragement. Remember that sharing experiences and exchanging coping strategies can help you feel less alone in your caregiving journey and offer new perspectives on managing challenges.
- **Be honest:** Acknowledge your limitations and recognize when you feel overwhelmed or stressed. It's okay to admit that you need help or are struggling to cope with the demands of caregiving. Being honest allows you to address your needs and prioritize self-care proactively.
- **Take breaks:** Schedule regular breaks throughout your day or week to rest, recharge, and engage in activities that bring you joy and relaxation. Whether taking a walk, reading a book, or practicing mindfulness, carving out time for self-care is essential for preventing burnout and maintaining your well-being.
- **Socialize:** Maintaining social connections with your friends, family, and community members is vital for your mental and emotional health. Make time to

attend social gatherings, events, or outings to
unwind, have fun, and connect with others.

- **Pay attention to your feelings and needs:** Check in
  with yourself regularly and pay attention to your
  emotions, physical sensations, and energy levels. If
  you're feeling stressed, exhausted, or overwhelmed,
  take steps to address your needs and prioritize self-
  care.

- **Take care of your health:** Maintaining physical
  health is crucial for managing stress and preventing
  burnout. Regular physical activity reduces stress,
  improves mood, and boosts energy levels. Find
  activities you enjoy, like walking, swimming, yoga, or
  dancing, and incorporate them into your daily
  routine. Aim for at least 30 minutes of moderate
  exercise most days of the week. Eat a balanced diet of
  fruits, vegetables, lean proteins, and whole grains.
  Stay hydrated, limit caffeine and alcohol intake, and
  avoid processed foods.

- **Maintain your sleep schedule:** Prioritize quality
  sleep by establishing a regular sleep schedule and
  creating a relaxing bedtime routine. Avoid caffeine,
  electronic devices, and stimulating activities before
  bed, and create a comfortable sleep environment.

- **Take leave:** Take time off from your caregiving
  duties. Taking a break from caregiving
  responsibilities can help prevent burnout, allow you
  to recharge, and focus on your well-being.

HEALTHY BOUNDARIES

As a caregiver, it's natural to want to provide unconditional support and assistance to your loved one. However, you may feel overwhelmed, resentful, or burnt out without clear boundaries. You need to set healthy boundaries to protect your overall health.

Some helpful tips that can help you to establish healthy boundaries include:

- **Let go of guilt:** Recognize that it's normal to feel guilty when setting boundaries, but understand that prioritizing your well-being is essential for effective caregiving. Remind yourself that taking care of yourself ultimately benefits you and your loved one. Practice self-compassion and remind yourself to do your best in a challenging situation.
- **Define and share your limits:** Identify your boundaries and communicate them clearly to your loved one and other involved parties. Whether it's regarding the type of care you can provide, the amount of time you can dedicate to caregiving, or specific tasks you're comfortable with, setting clear boundaries helps manage expectations and prevent resentment.
- **Take up a hobby:** Engaging in activities that bring you joy and fulfillment outside caregiving is essential for maintaining balance. Explore hobbies or interests you enjoy, whether painting, gardening, playing music, or participating in a sports team. Making time

for activities that nourish your soul helps reduce
stress and rejuvenate your spirit.

- **Set a schedule:** Establishing a structured caregiving
  schedule that includes regular breaks is crucial for
  preventing burnout and maintaining well-being.
  Plan specific times for daily caregiving tasks, self-
  care activities, and breaks. Stick to your schedule as
  much as possible to create a sense of routine and
  predictability.
- **Encourage your loved one's independence:**
  Empower them to maintain as much
  independence as possible by involving them in
  decision-making and encouraging self-care
  activities. Delegate tasks they can handle
  independently and provide support and
  encouragement as needed. Fostering
  independence promotes dignity and autonomy for
  your loved one while easing your caregiving
  responsibilities.
- **Plan for your absence:** Create a contingency plan
  when you cannot provide care due to illness, travel,
  or other commitments. Identify backup caregivers,
  respite care options, and emergency contacts to
  ensure continuity of care in your absence. Having a
  plan reduces stress and provides peace of mind for
  you and your loved one.
- **Tap into caregiver resources:** Take advantage of
  your community's caregiver resources and support
  services. Explore local organizations, online forums,
  support groups, and educational workshops
  designed specifically for caregivers. These resources
  provide valuable information, emotional support,

and practical assistance to help you navigate the challenges of caregiving.

SELF-CARE MATTERS

As a caregiver, your pivotal role demands dedication and care, embodying the selfless act of prioritizing your loved one's needs above your own. However, it's vital to recognize that neglecting your well-being can lead to burnout, ultimately diminishing your capacity to provide quality care. Remember, when your own cup is empty, effectively nurturing others becomes challenging.

Prioritizing self-care is essential to maintaining physical, emotional, and mental health. Your self-care can include simple activities like:

- getting regular exercise
- eating a healthy diet
- getting enough sleep
- soaking in a warm bath
- doing things that bring you joy and help you relax
- practicing mindfulness
- talking to trusted family or friends
- speaking to a therapist
- setting realistic expectations for yourself

Caregiving can be a challenging experience. However, it's essential to remember that you are not alone in this. Seeking support from your loved ones and friends or joining support groups can help you feel less isolated and provide emotional support.

Pay attention to your own needs and well-being amidst the demands of caregiving and whatever you do, and take the time to look after yourself. Here are some ideas on how you can start looking after yourself:

- **Reduce personal stress:** Identify sources of stress in your life and explore strategies to mitigate their impact. Practice relaxation techniques like deep breathing, meditation, or mindfulness to promote a sense of calm and reduce tension. Prioritize activities that bring you joy and relaxation, whether in nature, listening to music, or practicing a hobby.
- **Set goals:** Set realistic, achievable goals for yourself in your caregiving role and other areas of your life. Break your larger goals into smaller, manageable tasks, and celebrate your progress. Setting goals provides direction and motivation, helping you stay focused and empowered amidst the challenges of caregiving.
- **Seek solutions:** Approach caregiving challenges with a problem-solving mindset. Instead of dwelling on obstacles, brainstorm solutions and take proactive steps to address them. Collaborate with other family members, healthcare professionals, or community resources to explore innovative approaches and solve caregiving dilemmas effectively.
- **Communicate constructively:** Practice open, honest, and respectful communication with your loved one and others. Express your thoughts, feelings, and concerns assertively and listen actively to their perspective. Effective communication promotes understanding, strengthens relationships,

and fosters a sense of teamwork and collaboration in caregiving.

- **Ask for and accept help:** Recognize that it's okay to ask for help and accept support from others. Delegate tasks to your family members, friends, or hired caregivers to lighten your load and create more time for self-care. Be specific and communicate your needs clearly, allowing others to assist in meaningful ways.
- **Exercise:** Incorporate regular physical activity into your routine to improve overall health and well-being. Start with gentle exercises like walking, stretching, or yoga, and gradually increase intensity as you feel comfortable. Physical activity boosts mood, reduces stress, and enhances energy levels, making it an essential component of self-care for caregivers.
- **Learn from your emotions:** Always acknowledge and validate your emotions, recognizing that they're a natural response to the challenges of caregiving. Allow yourself to feel and express a range of emotions, whether frustration, sadness, or joy. Emotions provide valuable insights into your needs and experiences, and learning from them can help you cultivate greater self-awareness and resilience in your caregiving journey.

As a caregiver, it's vital to prioritize your own well-being. Ensuring your physical, emotional, and mental health is in check can help prevent burnout and compassion fatigue. Here are some ways to practice self-care: setting boundaries, seeking support from others, and dedicating time to activities that bring you joy and relaxation. Taking breaks, practicing mindfulness, and nurturing social connections are key components of self-care. By prioritizing your needs and showing yourself compassion, you'll be better equipped to provide quality care to your aging parents for the long haul.

This chapter explored various strategies for self-care. From reducing personal stress and setting goals to seeking solutions and communicating constructively, you were given tips to nurture your well-being amidst the demands of caregiving. By asking for help, talking to physicians, exercising, and learning from your emotions, you can empower yourself to prioritize self-care and sustain your ability to provide effective care to your loved ones.

As we conclude our journey through the intricacies of caregiving, we now focus on the importance of reflection and closure. Let's move on to explore the significance of acknowledging our experiences, celebrating our successes, and finding closure in our caregiving journey. Join us as we wrap up this transformative exploration, celebrating the resilience, compassion, and growth that define our caregiving experience.

CREATE A REVIEW!

Now that you have everything you need to confidently care for aging parents, it's time to share your newfound knowledge and show other readers where they can find the same help.

By sharing your honest opinion of this book on Amazon, you're not just leaving a review. You're influencing other caregivers, guiding them to the information they need, and igniting their passion for caring for aging parents.

Thank you for being so helpful. The family caregiving community is kept alive when we pass on our knowledge – and you're helping me to do just that.

Simply scan the QR code below to leave your review:

Leave a review!

CONCLUSION

Our 24-7 caregiver roles have been over for around three years now, and we both go to work in the morning and come home in the evening. We do a few things around the house daily and are actively involved in our church, attending services and meetings a few days per week. Not so long ago, we discussed how exhausted we felt after a particularly busy week, and we both agreed that our schedule was much easier than when we were taking care of Mike and Kay.

How could it have been possible for us to have more energy and endurance back then than we have now? The answer was simple: We took steps for self-care, asked for help when needed, made time for date nights, and prayed that God would provide what we needed for the moment. God was faithful and answered our prayers. Amid the difficulties, we could also enjoy sweet moments with Mike and Kay that we wouldn't trade for all the money in the world.

Whenever I hear Sam talk about it, one particular time brings a tear to my eye. Near the end of our journey, Mike was unable to get out of his wheelchair unassisted and unable to verbalize his thoughts. Sam had to lift him to get him to the restroom and bed.

At this point, Mike was unable to take steps on his own. Sam put Mike's feet on his own to walk him to the bed. The first time they did this, Sam remembered his childhood when he was about 5 or 6, and he used to walk around on top of his daddy's feet.

When Sam looked up at his father after placing his feet on his own, their eyes locked, and tears flowed. Sam said, "I remember, Dad. Do you remember?" Mike nodded and squeezed Sam tightly with a huge hug. This was one of the many sweet memories we hold dear and a priceless reward for walking this journey.

FINAL NOTE

Confidently Caring for Aging Parents is not just a book; it's a comprehensive road map, a guiding light if you want to navigate the intricate caregiving journey for your elderly loved ones. It delves into the multifaceted aspects of caring for aging parents, offering a wealth of insights, practical advice, and empathetic support to empower caregivers in their noble roles.

At the book's heart lies the C-C-C Care Approach—an ethos emphasizing compassion, communication, and collaboration. This approach is a cornerstone for effective caregiving, guiding caregivers to approach their responsibilities with kindness, openness, and teamwork.

Compassion is the first pillar of the C-C-C Care Approach. Caregiving is a deeply emotional journey, and approaching it with compassion allows caregivers to connect with their loved ones on a profound level. By understanding and empathizing with the challenges and emotions experienced by their aging parents, caregivers can provide support that is not only practical but also deeply meaningful.

Communication is the second pillar and is perhaps one of caregiving's most crucial aspects. Open and honest dialogue fosters understanding, strengthens relationships, and ensures that the needs and preferences of both the caregiver and the care recipient are heard and respected. Effective communication with healthcare professionals is vital for coordinating care, managing medical needs, and making informed decisions.

The third pillar, collaboration, underscores the importance of working with a support network. Caregiving is not a solitary endeavor; collaborating with family members, friends, healthcare professionals, and community resources can lighten the burden and enhance the quality of care. By leveraging their support network's collective expertise and resources, caregivers can navigate the challenges of caregiving more effectively.

Each chapter explores different facets of caregiving, offering practical advice, actionable strategies, and real-life examples to guide caregivers. From understanding the aging process and managing medical needs to navigating legal considerations and balancing work and caregiving responsibilities, the book covers various topics relevant to caregivers.

One of the book's key themes is the importance of self-care. Caregiving can be physically, emotionally, and mentally demanding, and neglecting one's well-being can lead to burnout and a diminished capacity to provide care effectively. *Confidently Caring for Aging Parents* encourages caregivers to prioritize self-care, offering strategies for managing stress, setting boundaries, and seeking support when needed.

Throughout the book, readers are encouraged to draw inspiration from the stories of resilience and triumph shared within its pages. These stories serve as reminders that while caregiving can be challenging, it is also deeply rewarding. They illustrate the transformative power of compassion, resilience, and the human spirit in overcoming adversity and finding strength in the face of adversity.

As caregivers immerse themselves in the wealth of information provided here, they gain the knowledge, skills, and confidence to navigate the complexities of caregiving with grace and resilience. They learn how to advocate for their loved ones, navigate the healthcare system, and provide holistic care that honors their aging parents' dignity and autonomy.

The book also emphasizes the importance of planning for the future. Aging is a natural part of life, and as our loved ones grow older, their care needs may evolve. *Confidently Caring for Aging Parents* encourages caregivers to discuss end-of-life wishes, advance care planning, and long-term care options, ensuring that their loved ones' wishes are honored and their needs are met with dignity and respect.

This book is a beacon of hope and guidance for caregivers facing the complex and challenging journey of caring for their elderly loved ones. Through its comprehensive approach, practical advice, and compassionate support, it empowers caregivers to navigate the ups and downs of caregiving with confidence, compassion, and unwavering determination. With the C-C-C Care Approach as their guide, caregivers can embark on this transformative journey knowing they have the knowledge, skills, and support to provide the best possible care for their aging parents while prioritizing their well-being.

REFERENCES

6 Ways to Help Older Adults Stay Physically Active as They Age. (2022, March 8). The Key. https://thekey.com/learning-center/6-ways-to-help-older-adults-stay-physically-active-as-they-age

7 Signs You Have Officially Become Your Loved Ones Caregiver. (n.d.). Hero. Retrieved April 26, 2024, from https://herohealth.com/blog/caregiving/7-signs-you-are-a-caregiver/

7 Steps for Hiring a Caregiver for In-Home Help. (n.d.). Daily Caring. Retrieved April 26, 2024, from https://dailycaring.com/7-steps-for-hiring-a-care giver-for-in-home-help/

Caregiver Burnout. (2023, August 16). Cleveland Clinic. https://my.cleveland clinic.org/health/diseases/9225-caregiver-burnout

Caregiver Guide: Mobility Problems. (n.d.). HealthInAging. https://www. healthinaging.org/tools-and-tips/caregiver-guide-mobility-problems

Caring for Aging Parents When You Can't Be There . (n.d.). Generations Senior Living. https://www.generationshcm.com/blog/2022/03/caring-for-parents-long-distance

Elderly Grooming: Tips When Bathing a Senior Loved One. (n.d.). Boundless Care. https://www.boundlesscare.org/elderly-grooming-tips-when-bathing-a-senior-loved-one

Fall prevention: Simple Tips to Prevent falls. (2022, February 3). Mayo Clinic. https://www.mayoclinic.org/healthy-lifestyle/healthy-aging/in-depth/fall-prevention/art-20047358

Falls and Fractures in Older Adults: Causes and Prevention. (2022, September 12). National Institute on Aging. https://www.nia.nih.gov/health/falls-and-falls-prevention/falls-and-fractures-older-adults-causes-and-prevention

Family Caregiving: Help and Support for Caregivers. (2019, March 21). Help-Guide. https://www.helpguide.org/articles/parenting-family/family-caregiving.htm

Galbreath, L. (2021, June 30). *Caring for the Mental Health of Older Adults.* Caregiving. https://www.caregiving.com/content/older-adults-mental-health-caregiving

Godman, H. (2022, February 28). *Taking an aging parent to the doctor? 10 helpful tips*. Harvard Health. https://www.health.harvard.edu/blog/taking-an-aging-parent-to-the-doctor-10-helpful-tips-202202282696

Habas, C. (2023, December 5). *5 Home Monitoring Systems for Senior Health and Safety*. National Council on Aging. https://www.ncoa.org/adviser/medical-alert-systems/best-elderly-monitoring-system-in-home-use/

How To Balance Work, FAMILY and Caregiving. (n.d.). The Caregiver Foundation. https://thecaregiverfoundation.org/learn-more/how-to-series/how-to-balance-work-family-and-caregiving

Huddleston, C. (2024, March 21). *Checklist for Managing Your Elderly Parents' Finances | Take Care*. Take Care. https://getcarefull.com/articles/checklist-for-taking-over-your-elderly-parents-finances

Jayson, S. (2019, October 28). *How to Make Your Home Safe for Aging Parents*. AARP. https://www.aarp.org/caregiving/home-care/info-2019/safety-tips.html

Kane, R. L. (2020, February 25). *How to Prepare to Become Your Parents' Caregiver*. Landmark Health. https://www.landmarkhealth.org/resource/how-to-prepare-to-become-your-parents-caregiver/

Lea, C. (n.d.). *Managing Medications for Aging Parents*. Mayo Clinic Health System. https://www.mayoclinichealthsystem.org/hometown-health/featured-topic/5-tips-for-managing-medications-for-aging-parents-during-a-pandemic

Longwell, C. (2020, November 11). *8 Expert Tips for Aging Parents That Won't Listen | The GreenFields*. The GreenFields Continuing Care Community | Lancaster, NY. https://thegreenfields.org/8-expert-tips-for-aging-parents-that-wont-listen/

Moyer, N. (2018, November 26). *How to Care for Yourself When You Have Caregiver Burnout*. Healthline; Healthline Media. https://www.healthline.com/health/health-caregiver-burnout

Orford, S. (2023, July 6). *9 Ways to Set Boundaries as a Caregiver*. Healthline. https://www.healthline.com/health/ways-to-set-boundaries-as-a-caregiver

Practical Solutions for Caregiver Stress. (2022, March 22). Mayo Clinic. https://www.mayoclinic.org/healthy-lifestyle/stress-management/in-depth/caregiver-stress/art-20044784

Renan. (2018, October 2). *Guide to Managing Elderly Parents' Medication in MD & DC*. SmithLife Homecare. https://www.smithlifehomecare.com/blog/managing-your-elderly-parents-medication/

Signs it Might be Time to Consider Aged Care for Your Parent. (2022, April 14).

Finley Regional Care. https://www.finleyregionalcare.com.au/signs-it-might-be-time-to-consider-aged-care-for-your-parent/

Stromberg, J. (2022, December 14). *Estate Planning Strategies for Your Aging Parents*. Divergent Planning. https://www.divergentplanning.com/blog/estate-planning-strategies-for-your-aging-parents

Taking Care of Yourself: Tips for Caregivers. (2023, October 12). National Institute on Aging. https://www.nia.nih.gov/health/caregiving/taking-care-yourself-tips-caregivers

Taylor, K. (2021, September 13). *What Can I Do About My Elderly Parent's Anxiety?* Family Choice Healthcare. https://familychoicehealthcare.com/blog/what-can-i-do-about-my-elderly-parents-anxiety

The Parkinson's Caregiver: 7 Ways to Help Your Loved One. (2019, November 19). Hopkins Medicine. https://www.hopkinsmedicine.org/health/conditions-and-diseases/parkinsons-disease/the-parkinsons-caregiver-7-ways-to-help-your-loved-one

Tips for Dealing with a Parent who has Dementia. (2022, August 31). Medical News Today. https://www.medicalnewstoday.com/articles/how-to-deal-with-dementia-parent

Tips for Supporting a Senior Who is Dealing with Delirium. (2019, January 29). Adara Home Health. https://adarahomehealth.com/tips-for-supporting-a-senior-who-is-dealing-with-delirium/

Vann, M. (2016, August). *The 15 Most Common Health Concerns for Seniors*. Everyday Health. https://www.everydayhealth.com/news/most-common-health-concerns-seniors/

Venson, A. H. (2022, June 15). *Coping with the Role Reversal when Caring for Aging Parents*. Multicultural Caregiving. https://multiculturalcaregiving.com/role-reversal-when-caring-for-aging-parents/

Ward, K. (2021, June 30). *18 Quick, Easy and Healthy Meals for Seniors*. Care. https://www.care.com/c/quick-easy-healthy-meals-for-seniors/

ABOUT THE AUTHOR

Meet Kim Livingston, a devoted wife, loving mother, and cherished grandmother whose commitment to her family profoundly shaped her life. Alongside her husband, Sam, she embraced the responsibility of caring for his aging parents, facing challenges that tested their resilience but also brought profound joy and strengthened their bonds.

Now, Kim shares her experiences through writing, aiming to offer support, guidance, and understanding to others navigating eldercare. Her motivation stems from the need she identified for support and understanding in the realm of eldercare.

Through her book, she hopes to illuminate the path for others and inspire a greater appreciation for the precious moments shared with loved ones in their twilight years. Kim's genuine desire to make a difference shines through with unwavering clarity and compassion, offering a beacon of support and understanding in the often-challenging caregiving journey.